The Twitter Presidency

T0174004

The Twitter Presidency explores the rhetorical style of President Donald J. Trump, attending to both his general manner of speaking as well as to his preferred modality. Trump's manner, the authors argue, reflects an aesthetics of white rage, and it is rooted in authoritarianism, narcissism, and demagoguery. His preferred modality of speaking, namely through Twitter, effectively channels and transmits the affective dimensions of white rage by taking advantage of the platform's defining characteristics, which include simplicity, impulsivity, and incivility. There is, then, a structural homology between Trump's general communication practices and the specific platform (Twitter) he uses to communicate with his base. This commonality between communication practices and communication platform (manner and modality) strikes a powerful emotive chord with his followers, who feel aggrieved at the decentering of white masculinity. In addition to charting the defining characteristics of Trump's discourse, *The Twitter Presidency* exposes how Trump's rhetorical style threatens democratic norms, principles, and institutions.

Brian L. Ott is Professor of Communication Studies and Director of the TTU Press at Texas Tech University, USA.

Greg Dickinson is Professor and Chair of Communication at Colorado State University, USA.

NCA Focus on Communication Studies

NATIONAL
COMMUNICATION
ASSOCIATION

The Twitter Presidency
Donald J. Trump and the Politics of White Rage
Brian L. Ott & Greg Dickinson

The Twitter Presidency

Donald J. Trump and the Politics of White Rage

Brian L. Ott and Greg Dickinson

Routledge
Taylor & Francis Group

NEW YORK AND LONDON

First published 2019
by Routledge
52 Vanderbilt Avenue, New York, NY 10017

and by Routledge
2 Park Square, Milton Park, Abingdon, Oxon OX14 4RN

First issued in paperback 2020

Routledge is an imprint of the Taylor & Francis Group, an informa business

© 2019 Taylor & Francis

The right of Brian L. Ott and Greg Dickinson to be identified as authors of this work has been asserted by them in accordance with sections 77 and 78 of the Copyright, Designs and Patents Act 1988.

Library of Congress Cataloging in Publication Data
A catalog record has been requested for this book

ISBN 13: 978-0-367-67028-3 (pbk)
ISBN 13: 978-0-367-14975-8 (hbk)

Typeset in Sabon
by Apex CoVantage, LLC

Contents

Tables

Preface

This book is about President Donald J. Trump and, more specifically, about President Trump's rhetoric, which includes both his general manner of speaking (what Carol Anderson (2016), in a different context, has called, "white rage") and his preferred modality of speaking (i.e., through Twitter). It is, in short, a book about his *rhetorical style*. Our central aim throughout this book is to identify the defining traits of that rhetorical style, to explain how it functions, and to reflect on its consequentiality. As we do so, however, it is crucial to understand that this style is not, in fact, *his*. In other words, it is not unique to President Trump. He did not invent the politics of white rage or even popularize its open expression on the platform of Twitter. So, no matter how obviously he may embody this style (and embody it he does!), it would be misguided to suggest that the president created it.

A rhetorical style is, after all, a pattern, a culturally "stylized" way (i.e., a manner and modality) of speaking. Rather than merely being a single person's way of speaking, a rhetorical style reflects a much broader confluence of cultural, political, and technological factors. While such factors contributed to Trump's political success, they existed prior to and independent of him. Therefore, Trump's rhetoric is best understood as an extension (not source) of three social forces: (1) fear and anxiety over the perceived decentering of white masculinity; (2) the formal properties of social media platforms; and (3) the deleterious state of the news media (represented most obviously by Fox News). Trump did *not* create these contexts; he simply became a key inflection point for their collective expression, for he offered a particularly clear, consistent, and compelling performance of their underlying affects.

To acknowledge that the politics of white rage, the structural logics of Twitter and other social media platforms, and the de-evolution of news into entertainment (24-hour cable news) did not originate with Donald Trump is in no way to excuse the president from the very real dangers created by his reliable performance of a rhetorical style rooted in these forces. Simply stated, Trump's rhetoric makes him the most dangerous person ever elected president of the United States. He is dangerous for a multitude of reasons, but most notably because—like other authoritarians and demagogues—Trump continuously seeks to consolidate power, which he does through divisive scapegoating, disregard for democratic norms, and ubiquitous and unashamed lying. Far from becoming "more presidential," as Trump promised he would be if elected, his rhetoric has become uglier, less egalitarian, and more deceptive since taking office.

The frequency of his lying, for instance, is on the rise. As the *Washington Post* reported, President Trump averaged 4.9 false and misleading claims per day during his first 100 days in office, but that number has grown steadily (Kessler et al., 2017). As of August 1, 2018, his average number of false statements per day had risen to 7.6, and during the months of June and July, Trump averaged 16 false and misleading statements per day (Kessler et al., 2018). Trump's propensity for lying is so prolific that one of the most reliable predictors of truth in the contemporary political landscape is that the president has asserted its opposite. How, then, does one seriously analyze Trump's rhetoric when much of what he says is blatantly untrue? This is, in part, why it is critical to focus on style. It emphasizes not so much *what* he says, but the *way* (i.e., the manner and modality) he says it, and the way Trump says things is, at once, dangerous and consequential. As such, in addition to highlighting the defining elements of this style, another aim of this book is to identify the real, material harms associated with its enactment.

The harms associated with Trump's rhetoric cannot, however, be blamed exclusively on his hyper-masculine bullying and insult-laden tweeting. A long list of persons and groups are complicit in his dangerous rhetoric, including his sycophantic staff (Sarah Huckabee Sanders, Mike Pence, Kellyanne Conway, Stephen Miller, John Kelly, Ivanka Trump, etc.), the cowardly Republicans in Congress who endorse his destructive and divisive politics (Paul Ryan, Mitch McConnell, Devin Nunes, etc.), the talking heads who repeat his idiotic ideas endlessly on political entertainment shows like *Hannity* and *Fox & Friends* (Rudy Giuliani, Sebastian Gorka, etc.), the pseudo-news personalities who feed his conspiratorial fantasies (Sean Hannity, Jeanine Pirro, Laura Ingram, etc.), the alt-right and neo-Nazi movements, the Russian government, and, of course, Trump followers.

To be clear, there is a significant difference between "Trump voters" (i.e., those persons who unwittingly acted as agents of the Russian government by casting their vote for Trump in 2016, but who have no particular allegiance to or even affinity for him) and "Trump followers" (i.e., those persons who blindly support Trump, parroting his racist remarks, ridiculous lies, and absurd conspiracy theories). We have designated them "followers" rather than "supporters" due to their mindless, cult-like response to Trump, as well as the use of the moniker in social media contexts such as Twitter. Trump's followers are "true believers" in Eric Hoffer's sense of that term (Pies 2017); they feel their lives are "irredeemably spoiled" and, thus, have sacrificed their sense of autonomy (and their capacity for independent, critical thought) to a larger movement. "A rising mass movement attracts and holds a following not by its doctrines and promises," Hoffer (1951) notes, "but by the refuge it offers from the anxieties, barrenness and meaninglessness of an individual existence" (39). The first group, Trump voters, exercised poor judgment, and we invite them to see and confront that error in judgment. The second group, Trump followers, are driven not so much by poor judgment as they are by poor self-worth, which they collectively express in the denigration of (racial) others.

To some, the preceding paragraph may seem harsh. However, it is crucial to acknowledge that Donald Trump could not have undermined our national character or eroded the principles, norms, and institutions of American democracy to the degree that he is without considerable aid from others. The evangelical right is especially deserving of admonishment for their hypocritical support of a president and an administration that demonstrate such contempt for truth, justice, ethics, and basic human decency.[1] All of that is by way of saying that we refuse to hide our disgust and outrage regarding Trump's toxic rhetoric and its material dangers behind the polite, pseudo-objective tone of academic prose. While we are committed to a rigorous analysis of his rhetoric, we will not pretend that there is a reasonable response to such discourse that does not forcefully condemn its underlying racism, sexism, homophobia, and nationalist xenophobia. We, along with every US citizen, have an ethical obligation to hold the president accountable for his demeaning, detestable, and deceitful discourse.

Having outlined the basic contours of our project, we wish to say a few words about how it arose. This book started with the publication of an essay titled "The Age of Twitter: Donald J. Trump and the Politics of Debasement," which appeared in vol. 34, no. 1 of *Critical Studies in Media Communication* (2017). Based on the essay's success,

Brian was contacted by the Publications Board of the National Communication Association to see if he had any interest in expanding the essay into a book-length study. Since he was already working on a separate piece with Greg about Trump and white rage, a book-length project seemed like a perfect opportunity to examine Trump's rhetoric through a broader lens, one that combined an analysis of Trump's affective appeal with an analysis of the medium through which that affect was largely mobilized. The rest is, as they say, history. Here is how we plan to proceed.

Overview of Chapters

Chapter 1, "Situating Trump," seeks to locate the study of Trump's discursive and communicative practices in the appropriate academic literatures. It begins by examining the scholarship on style, highlighting the fundamentally rhetorical, political, and collective character of style. It then examines the history of political campaign communication and presidential rhetoric, paying special attention to the role social media plays in contemporary politics. As it synthesizes the literature in these areas, it reviews the rapidly growing body of literature on Trump's campaign and presidency. It concludes by arguing for the importance of attending both to the uniquely affective appeal of his rhetorical style, which is rooted in an aesthetic of white rage, and to his preferred modality of communication, Twitter, which the president expertly mobilized to achieve maximum affective effect (reach and influence).

Chapter 2, "The Politics of White Rage," explores how Trump's brand of politics appeals to voters not because of its ideology or policy positions but because of its affective resonances. Specifically, it argues that Trump utilizes an aesthetic of white rage, a rhetorical style animated largely by fears and anxieties about the decentering of White masculinity. This style, we further argue, is evident across his managerial, physical, and linguistic performances. While Twitter offered the president a new modality for communicating white rage, it is crucial to recognize that the aesthetics of white rage are old and deep, rooted in the slave trade, and woven into the nation's fabric. Understanding the ways that Trump's rhetoric expresses, particularly on an affective level, this already available racist aesthetic begins to explain why counter-appeals to logic and reason constantly fail to combat it. Engaging this rhetoric at the aesthetic and affective registers will be the only way to undermine its power.

Chapter 3, "Trump Tweets," explores how Trump's rhetorical style was well suited to the defining characteristics of Twitter as a social media platform. It is based upon, or more accurately "inspired by," a previously published essay on Trump's use of Twitter during the campaign. It significantly revises that essay, however, by expanding its historical scope to include Trump's use of Twitter as a citizen, as a candidate, and as president. While we argue there is a certain consistency in Trump's Twitter habits over time, mostly notable in his tonality and temperament, there are also key differences. Early on, Trump employed Twitter principally for self-branding, self-promotion, and airing personal grievances. As he transitioned into the role of candidate, Trump's tweeting became tactical, focusing on message repetition, unconventional use of the platform to disrupt political norms, and aggressive and demeaning attacks on his Republican challengers and Hilary Clinton. Finally, following the election, Trump's Twitter habits shifted again, reflecting a strategic set of practices designed to promote his distorted, self-involved view of reality, to distract from potentially harmful news stories and investigations, and to discredit the mainstream news media as well as other perceived threats through persistent and perfunctory attacks.

Chapter 4, "In Defense of Democracy," outlines how Trump's rhetorical style—in both manner and modality—gravely threatens American democracy, attending to the ways in which it undermines civility and degrades the level of political discourse in the U.S., erodes democratic norms and institutions, weakens the rule of law, fuels racial hatred and fosters discrimination, favors anti-intellectualism and undermines critical thought, and promotes mistrust of the mainstream news media and facilitates a post-truth politics. To combat the material harms of Trump's rhetoric, the chapter ends with a call for mobilizing reasonable disgust at Trump's affective politics of white rage to realize a more progressive politics rooted in James Baldwin's radical understanding of love.

Acknowledgments

This, like all books, is a corporate project. Rob Brookey provided the initial impetus for the book with his invitation to Brian to write a short essay for *Critical Studies in Media Communication*. The success of that essay led to the invitation from Felisa Salvago Keyes at Routledge to expand that essay into a short book and we want to thank Felisa for her direction at the early stages of this project. We want to thank in particular the work of Jordin Clark a doctoral student at Colorado State University. Jordin played a number of roles in building this book including conducting a careful search of all Trump's Twitter posts as well as gathering many of the videoed Trump speeches starting with his candidacy announcement. She also provided invaluable help in transforming our various citations into Harvard style. The book simply would not have been published without her help.

Note

1. "[M]ore than 80% of white evangelicals voted for the Trump–Pence ticket" (Burke 2018).

References

Anderson, C. 2016. *White rage: The unspoken truth of our racial divide*. New York: Bloomsbury.

Burke, D. 2018. Why some evangelicals don't want Vice President Pence to speak at their meeting, *CNN.com* [online]. Available at: https://edition.cnn.com/2018/06/13/politics/mike-pence-southern-baptist-convention-speech/index.html [Accessed 20 August 2018].

Hoffer, E. 1951. *The true believer: Thoughts on the nature of mass movements*. New York: Harper & Row.

Kessler, G., Lee, M., and Kelly, M. 2017. President Trump's first six months: The fact-check tally, *The Washington Post* [online]. Available at: www.washingtonpost.com/news/fact-checker/wp/2017/07/20/president-trumps-first-six-months-the-fact-check-tally/?utm_term=.11d1a68144da [Accessed 20 August 2018].

Kessler, G., Rizzo, S., and Kelly, M. 2018. President Trump has made 4,229 false or misleading claims in 558 days. *The Washington Post* [online]. Available at: www.washingtonpost.com/news/fact-checker/wp/2018/08/01/president-trump-has-made-4229-false-or-misleading-claims-in-558-days/?utm_term=.2cf8b56613e5 [Accessed 20 August 2018].

Ott, B.L. 2017. The age of Twitter: Donald J. Trump and the politics of debasement. *Critical Studies in Media Communication*, 34(1), pp. 59–68.

Pies, R.W. 2017. Inside the minds of Trump's 'true believers.' *The Conversation* [online]. Available at: http://theconversation.com/inside-the-minds-of-trumps-true-believers-79986 [Accessed 20 August 2018].

1 Situating Trump

In his 1935 novel *It Can't Happen Here*, Nobel Prize-winning author Sinclair Lewis stories the unlikely political rise of Berzelius "Buzz" Windrip, whose angry rhetoric, populist platform, and anti-foreigner sentiment win him the US presidency. A number of commentators have, of course, drawn parallels between the story of Windrip, a cautionary tale about fascism, and the 2016 election of Donald J. Trump (Harris 2015; Beale 2016; Stewart 2017). Frankly, it is hard not to, especially given Lewis's (1935) uncanny depiction of Windrip as "vulgar, almost illiterate, a public liar easily detected, and in his 'ideas' almost idiotic" (p. 86). But perhaps most presciently of all, Lewis (1935) observes that, in addition to being a master entertainer, Windrip possesses an "uncommon natural ability to be authentically excited by and with his audience, and they by and with him" (p. 87). It is no exaggeration to say that Trump genuinely *excited*—a term that signals his distinctively affective appeal—a significant segment of the American electorate, or to note that he did so and continues to do so in spite of an overwhelming array of obstacles. Consider what we know.

Despite having no prior political experience, despite being temperamentally unfit (LeTourneau 2017), psychologically unstable (Bulman 2017; Gartner 2017; Morris 2017), a sexist (Cohen 2017; Robbins 2017), a racist (Milbank 2015; Coates 2017; Marcotte 2017a; O'Connor 2017), a xenophobe (Milbank 2016), a conspiracy theorist (Cillizza 2017a; Marcotte 2017), and a serial liar (Cillizza 2017b; Kessler et. al 2017; *Los Angeles Times* 2017; Moye 2017), and despite having committed grave missteps—missteps that would have surely ended a more conventional candidacy—during the campaign (Kirk et al. 2016; Kruse and Gee 2016), Trump eked out a narrow electoral victory to become the 45th president of the United States. At the much-hyped 100-day mark of his presidency, despite failing to accomplish or even advance many of his signature campaign promises (i.e., to repeal Obamacare and to build a wall on the southern border) and reversing himself on others (i.e., NATO and labeling China a currency manipulator) (Garrett 2017), 96 percent of those who voted for him still supported him (Langer 2017). And perhaps most remarkably that support continued largely unabated even after President Trump began to be investigated for obstructing justice in the FBI's investigation into his campaign's potential collusion with a foreign power to influence the outcome of the 2016 US presidential election (Tesfamichael 2017).

Given the unwavering loyalty of his base, one cannot help but wonder what makes Trump so appealing to his followers. Understanding this appeal is the province of rhetoric and, thus, rhetorical scholars are uniquely well positioned and equipped to assess Trump's improbable political success. But doing so effectively requires an approach as unconventional as President Trump himself, for his appeal cannot be accounted for through reference to traditional categories or modes of analysis. In fact, as a preliminary critical step, it is useful to eliminate a few well-known rhetorical appeals. Trump's success lies not in well-reasoned arguments, as he is clearly neither articulate nor cogent.[1] His appeal lies not in his moral character or trustworthiness, as he is ethically bereft and behaves with utter disregard for the truth.[2] Finally, his appeal lies not in his beliefs or policy positions, as he demonstrates no allegiance to either (Shapiro 2016). Indeed, post-election surveys of Trump's supporters confirm these suppositions.[3] But if conventional factors such as rational discourse, personal ethos, and ideological disposition offer little basis for understanding Trump's rhetorical appeal, then what explains it?

We maintain throughout this book that it is primarily Trump's style. In fact, style may be the only aspect of Trump's rhetoric consistent enough to account for his appeal. Reflecting on the first five months of the Trump presidency, Rich Lowry (2017) observed for *Politico*, "the only . . . unquestioned constant is Trump's demeanor. Or to put it another way, Trump's content may be subject to change, but never his style." Consequently, our chief aim in this book is to explicate and assess Trump's material embodiment and enactment of an emergent populist style, which drawing inspiration from Carol Anderson (2016), we refer to as "white rage." For us, style combines Trump's general manner of speaking with his preferred modality of speaking. To ensure that each of these elements receives adequate attention, we analyze Trump's rhetorical style across both registers. In Chapter 2, we focus on the affective appeal of white rage, and in Chapter 3, we focus on the president's unprecedented use of Twitter to widely transmit this affective appeal. But before turning to our specific analysis of Trump's rhetoric, it is crucial to ground our analysis in the extant literature on style, campaign communication, and presidential discourse, as well as to highlight the stakes of the president's rhetorical style.

On Style

Style is a complex and challenging concept to define. Part of the difficulty arises from the fact that everything from clothing and cars to writing and speech is infused with style, which in the broadest sense refers to the observable aesthetic qualities or patterns of discourses, objects, events, and practices. Style, in other words, describes the "social appearance" of things or, in the words of media scholar Stuart Ewen (1996), "[the manner in which] human values, structures, and assumptions in a given society are aesthetically expressed and received" (p. 3). Ewen's definition is a helpful one, as it implicitly highlights that style is expressly rhetorical, overtly political, and manifestly collective. In this section, we explore each of these features in greater depth as a way of situating the analysis of Donald Trump and his discourse that follows in Chapters 2 and 3.

Rhetorical Character

Style has long been regarded as one of the traditional canons of rhetoric along with invention, organization, memory, and delivery, and Aristotle treated it extensively in both his *Rhetoric* and *Poetics*. In the classical context, style largely "meant strategic language choice and embellishment of discourse" (Brummett 2016). But over time, the concept has evolved to describe "the aesthetic dimension of communication" more generally (Brummett 2009, p. 249). This includes not only linguistic traits, but also embodied movement, gestures, and nonverbal expression, as well as fashion and appearance. To this list, we would add managerial and leadership behaviors, which in the case of Trump are exceedingly autocratic and authoritarian, and overall deportment or manner, which for Trump we would characterize as obnoxious, overbearing, and oblivious.

While scholars typically do not talk about style as involving a substantive message, it is rhetorical because it conveys a general sensibility about, disposition toward, or way of being-in-the-world. As such, in contrast to more traditional understandings of discourse, the rhetorical dimensions of style are rooted in aesthetic expression and direct sensory experience rather than symbolicity and representational systems of thought. Style, in the words of Bradford Vivian (2002), "is an aesthetic (rather than conceptual) rhetoric; an affective (not rational) communication" (p. 238). Therefore, style is best approached not in terms of meaning and message, but in terms of meaningfulness and mood, i.e., its capacity for transmitting intensive forces and atmospheric-like qualities between and among bodies.

Style, in short, functions affectively. The scholarship on affect is dominated by two major paradigms. The first, which has its roots in psychology and neuroscience, regards affect as an elemental state, i.e., a manifest emotion such as fear or joy, elicited in a human subject by an external stimulus. The second, which draws upon philosophy and more humanistic disciplines, views affect as a prepersonal intensity, i.e., a productive force, that all bodies—whether human or not—exert upon one another as they move and interact. It is this second conception of affect, as productive force, that informs our understanding of style. In this view, affect works to excite, prime, and sway "bodies at a material, presubjective, asignifying level" (Ott 2017, p. 10) by either augmenting or diminishing their state of capacitation.[4] Extending this point, Brian Massumi (2015) observes that the body's capitation "is completely bound up with the lived past of the body" (p. 49), meaning that how the body responds to an affective invitation depends upon that body's memories and tendencies, a fact that has tremendous heuristic potential for explaining the dramatically polarized responses to Trump and his performance of white rage.

Affect, in this view, is a dynamic, inter-relational force produced between and among bodies, all of which bear traces of past lived experience. In treating society as a process rather than a structure, this conception of affect honors Gilles Deleuze and Felix Guattari's radical idea that "*There is no ideology, and never was*" (Deleuze and Guattari 1988, cited in Massumi 2015, p. 84). Understood as asignifying, presubjective, and non-ideological, affect is a "more fundamental concept than rationality," a concept that "*pertains more fundamentally to events than to persons*" (Massumi 2015, p. 91). Such a view is particularly well suited to aid in understanding and assessing an emergent political style, especially as embodied and enacted by someone who has been described as a non-ideological pragmatist and "ideology-free populist" (Schneider 2017; see also Scalia 2016; Schmitt 2016). To claim that affect is nonideological is not to suggest that it is not concerned with power. On the contrary, explains Massumi (2015), "Power comes up into us from the field of potential. . . . It's the calculable part of affect, the most probable next steps and eventual outcomes" (p. 19). We will expand upon this understanding of affect in the following chapter.

Political Character

In asserting that style mobilizes "affective responses to change or stabilize the existing distribution of power," James Aune (2008, p. 483)
highlights that style is political as well as rhetorical in character. One
of the earliest attempts to grapple with style as political is Richard
Hoftsadter's (1965) essay "The Paranoid Style in American Politics,"
which he delivered as the Herbert Spencer Lecture at Oxford in 1963.
Hoftsadter opens his essay noting that American political life has
"served again and again as an arena for uncommonly angry minds"
(p. 3). Citing the Goldwater movement at the time as an example of
this fact, he argues that behind such movements is a "style of mind."
Dubbing it the "paranoid style," he claims it reflects "the qualities
of heated exaggeration, suspiciousness, and conspiratorial fantasy"
(p. 3). Hoftsadter is careful not to associate the paranoid style with
a single political party or ideology, and he finds elements of this style
in prairie populism, McCarthyism, Illuminism, and Masonry. Among
Hofstadter's many insights is that the paranoid style entails a widely
shared political sentiment or sensibility, though it may be affiliated
with a particular spokesperson in a given context.

Style, however, is not only helpful in engaging modes of political
address that we can judge as deleterious. For Robert Hariman (1995),
"style is a significant dimension of every human experience" (p. 4),
including civic and political life. Arguing that the analysis of politics must take account of "the role of sensibility, taste, manners, . . .
and similarly compositional and performative qualities," Hariman
(1995, p. 4) defines political style as *"a coherent repertoire of rhetorical conventions depending on aesthetic responses for political effect"*
(p. 4). Utilizing this definition, Hariman unpacks four political styles,
which he labels realist, courtly, republican, and bureaucratic. Based
on a careful analysis of these styles across archetypical texts, Hariman
concludes that we must rethink understandings of power that reduce
it to the exercise of individual agency and coercive force in favor of
socially negotiated relations constituted through aesthetic expressions
and their interpretation (p. 189).

Drawing upon the work of Hofstadter, Hariman, and others, Benja-
min Moffitt (2016) examines the matter of populism. Rejecting previous
attempts to theorize populism in terms of ideology, strategy, discourse,
and logic, Moffitt argues that populism is best conceptualized as a
distinctive political style. Studying 28 populist leaders from around
the globe, Moffitt distills the political style of populism into three key
features: an appeal to "the people" versus "the elite," "bad manners"

in language, embodied movement, and clothing, and the performance of crisis, breakdown, or threat (pp. 41–45). In each instance, Moffitt maintains that a populist political style can be counter-posed with a technocratic political style. So, for instance, while populists appeal to the wisdom and common sense of the people, technocrats defer to experts and specialists; while populists exercise bad manners, technocrats present themselves in a more formal fashion; while populists invoke the specter of crisis, technocrats appeal to stability or measured progress (Moffitt 2016, pp. 46–47). In light of this dichotomy, which refers not "to modes of governance or ideological dispositions, but to *distinct embodied, performative political styles*" (Moffitt 2016, p. 47), it is not hard to see why Trump ran against and continues, nearly two years later, to juxtapose himself with Barack Obama.

Collective Character

A third crucial feature of style is its collective character, its capacity to not only to function as a marker of "social and cultural allegiance" (Brummett 2016, p. 7), but also as the productive force behind shared sentiments and sensibilities. In fact, scholars have been critical of accounts such as Hariman's delineation of political styles for associating style too strongly with "the reasoned . . . decisions of a humanist agent," thereby reducing it to "rational, purposeful communication" (Vivian 2002, p. 225). Drawing upon Michel Maffesoli's reconception of style, Vivian (2002) emphasizes that "style 'allows and enables liaison among all the members of a society' according to the dissemination of certain cultural aesthetics, which have become, in many social situations, a more serviceable cultural 'language' than democratic deliberation" (p. 235).

In keeping with this view, it should be remembered that the populist political style embodied by Trump neither originated with nor was, in any sense, "authored" by him; rather "Trump's style" is simply his performance or aesthetic expression of a more widely shared "language" or sensibility.

This clarification is significant because it helps account for the manner in which a style may connect and bond individuals who hold otherwise discordant political views. "Collective sentiments and aesthetic rituals," elaborates Vivian (2002), "influence novel social alliances, affinities between markedly different groups, by virtue of the ways in which they are publicly expressed, performed, or symbolized" (p. 237). This seems especially relevant in the case of Trump who managed to appeal to voters with disparate views on many political issues.

What mobilized Trump voters was a shared sensibility, not about the economy, as popular perception has it (on the contrary, "financially troubled voters in the white working class were more likely to prefer Clinton"), but about "feeling like a stranger in America" (Green 2017). In short, racial anxiety trumped economic anxiety as a predictor of support for Trump in the 2016 US presidential election (McElwee and McDaniel 2017). This, of course, cut both ways; even as Trump's populist performance of "white rage" appealed to some voters, it strongly alienated and even mobilized others in opposition (Barabak 2017). We explore this phenomenon in much greater detail in Chapter 2, but, first, it is important to situate Trump's rhetoric in the context of political campaign communication and presidential discourse.

On Political Communication

In the second edition of *Uncivil Wars*, Thomas A. Hollihan (2009), Professor in the Annenberg School for Communication at the University of Southern California, writes, "Politics is fundamentally a communicative activity" (p. 9). As such, the study of politics is, at its core, the study of communication: (1) of how political elites—elected and appointed officials, party leaders, lobbyists, etc.—rally public support for their positions and policies through persuasive efforts; (2) of how media professionals report on politicians and political issues; and (3) of how citizens express their support or dissent for candidates, officeholders, the media, and other relevant stakeholders. While the scholarship on political communication employs a diverse array of approaches and perspectives to examine all three of these dimensions, our focus in this study is on two specific types of political discourse: campaign communication and presidential rhetoric. In this section, we review some of the key research in these two areas as a way of situating the analysis of Trump that follows.

Campaign Communication

Research on political campaign communication is rooted in the premise that important differences mark the rhetoric of campaigning and the rhetoric of governing. First, as Hugh Heclo (2000) explains, whereas campaigning seeks to influence a single decision, i.e., which candidate to vote for at an "unambiguous decision point in time," governing aims at influencing a "line of decision" over time (p. 11). Second, given the "fixed time horizon" of an election, "campaigning is necessarily adversarial [while . . .] governing is primarily collaborative"

(Heclo 2000, p. 12). In light of these key features, which have "winning an election" as their principal goal, "Political campaign discourse is therefore unquestionably instrumental, or functional, in nature" (Benoit, 2007, p. 32). Adopting a functional perspective, which assumes (1) that voting is a comparative act, (2) that candidates must distinguish themselves from their opponents, and (3) that campaign communication allows candidates to distinguish themselves, William Benoit (2007) argues political campaign discourse is typically characterized by three functions (acclaiming, attacking, and defending) and two topics (policy and character).

The first function of political campaign communication is *acclaiming*, which entails speech aimed at enhancing the reputation of the speaker through self-praise (Benoit 2001, p. 114). Common subjects of acclaim or "positive self-presentation" include past accomplishments, previous experience, and desirable personal traits (Benoit et al., 1997: 5). Trump, for instance, engaged in acclaiming by repeatedly touting his business background and tough negotiation skills during the 2016 campaign. The second function of campaign discourse is *attacking*, or speech that seeks to highlight an opponent's weaknesses. As with acclaiming, the content of attacking usually focuses on either policy considerations or personal character. While attacking in political campaigns is not at all unique to Trump, what was unique was the especially nasty, personal, and demeaning nature of his attacks. As Oscar Winberg (2017) contends, Trump's rhetoric replaced attack politics with insult politics. *Defending*, the third key function of campaign communication, refers to the manner in which candidates refute accusations and engage in image repair. Trump, like prior political candidates, frequently had to defend himself against attacks, and he employed common strategies such as denial, evasion, and minimization to do so. One strategy noticeably absent from Trump's rhetorical toolbox, however, was apologia, as Trump obviously regards it as a sign of weakness.

In addition to a concern with the rhetorical function of campaign discourse, research has also investigated how political campaigns have changed over time. Though they vary somewhat in their terminological preferences, scholars typically divide political campaign communication into three historical stages: premodern, modern, and postmodern (Farrell 1996, p. 170). Each of these stages is characterized by a guiding paradigm, dominant medium of communication, and particular type of messaging. The premodern campaign, for instance, generally entailed a party logic; it was conducted through partisan newspapers and radio broadcasts, and conveyed a party-line message. The modern campaign, by contrast, reflected a media logic; it was waged largely on national television and the evening news, and targeted a mass audience through images, sound bites, and impression management. Finally, the postmodern campaign is driven by a marketing logic; it operates in a digital environment that includes niche television and social media, and employs narrow-casting and micro-messaging to target specific voters (Strömbäck and Kiousus 2014, p. 117). Given broad acceptance of this typology, contemporary political campaign research often focuses on postmodern campaigns and the specific ways candidates operate in that unique media environment.

Candidates for public office utilize a wide range of modalities for conveying their values and policy objectives, including public speeches and rallies, press conferences and press releases, candidate debates, appearances on television, public mailings, radio and TV advertisements, Web pages, social media, recorded telephone messages, canvasing, yard signs, buttons, bumper stickers, and personal actions (Benoit 2007, p. 64; Hollihan 2009, p. 9). But in the postmodern era, presidential campaigns are dominated by television and social media. While this trend continued in the 2016 presidential campaign, Trump utilized television in several nontraditional ways and demonstrated a remarkable ability to create synergy between television and social media. In the remainder of this section, we review key literature on media use in political campaigns, as well as some of the rapidly emerging scholarship of Trump's unique implementation of media during the 2016 presidential campaign.

While presidential debates and national party conventions are important and certainly heavily viewed televisual events, TV's primary impact on presidential political campaigns has traditionally come in the form of 30- and 60-second advertising spots. As Kathleen Hall Jamieson wrote in 1996:

> Political advertising is now the major means by which candidates for the presidency communicate their messages to voters. As a conduit of this advertising, television attracts both more candidate dollars and more audience attention than radio or print. Unsurprisingly, the spot ad is the most used and the most viewed of the available forms of advertising.
>
> (p. 517)

Research generally shows that television spots influence voters (Benoit 2007, p. 68), and that the more candidates spend on TV spots the more influence they buy. So, on first glance, the fact that Hillary Clinton's campaign spent more than $1 billion on television advertising, nearly twice as much as Trump's campaign, defies conventional wisdom. But there are some crucial mitigating factors to consider. First, while Clinton spent more money than Trump on television advertising, she spent significantly less than Obama did in the previous two races. Second, Clinton did not advertise widely in key Rust Belt states such as Wisconsin and Michigan until the final week of the campaign (Stein 2017). Trump, by contrast, spent more on television advertising in Michigan in just the month of September than either 2012 presidential campaign (Obama or Romney) spent during the entire election cycle (Mauger n.d.). Third, Clinton's TV ads focused more on character than policy, which was a departure from previous election cycles (Parry-Giles et al. 2017).

Post-election analysis of Trump's campaign suggests a number of key findings. While Trump spent less total money on television ad buys, his spending was more electorally targeted and likely more effective. Perhaps more importantly, the Trump campaign utilized television in several nontraditional ways that appear to have been more effective than TV ad buys. Trump, for instance, regularly held large, raucous campaign rallies, many of which CNN aired in full during the primary season. In addition, he regularly phoned into political entertainment programs on Fox News, who put him on the air. Finally, Trump regularly tweeted "highly acerbic remarks, putdowns, and accusations" on Twitter (Johnson 2017, p. xiv) that were, in turn, widely reported on and analyzed by television "news" outlets.[5] These three strategies significantly amplified Trump's message and media presence, earning him by some estimates $5 billion worth campaign coverage (Broder 2017). So, while "Hillary Clinton held enormous advantages in fund-raising and television advertising expenditures . . . it was Trump who ultimately won more exposure in news coverage and social media" (Francia 2017, p. 2). Given Trump's success in generating unpaid advertising, it is worth examining more closely how he manipulated news coverage and mobilized Twitter toward this end.

Having spent years as the star of his own reality television series, Trump understood the storytelling and image-making power of television, and he leveraged the central logics of reality television— (1) sensationalism, (2) promotionalism (self-branding and reputation-seeking), and (3) "authenticity," which is figured primarily through the lens of "emotional transparency"—to influence the agenda of the news media. In routinely making outrageous statements on pseudo-news programs, during presidential debates, and at circus-like campaign rallies, Trump seized the logic of spectacle and sensationalism to generate unprecedented free news coverage (Hearn 2016). As Francia (2017) recounts:

> Trump's most sizable exposure advantage over Clinton came in the form of news stories. A full 43% of likely voters in June and another 40% in August reported that they saw more news stories of Trump than they did about Clinton. By comparison, just 12% of likely voters in June and 13% in August reported that they saw more news stories of Clinton than they did about Trump, providing Trump with a net advantage of 31 percentage points and 27 percentage points in June and August, respectively. Consistent with previous results and FMT expectations, Trump topped Clinton in unpaid media exposure.
>
> (p. 11)

Moreover, Trump took advantage of reality TV's neoliberal grammar of promotionalism to establish "the rogue businessman as a new kind of expert and leader extraordinaire" (Oullette 2016, p. 649). Finally, "appearing bellicose, off-the-cuff, and spontaneous," he fostered an image of emotional authenticity, one that mirrors reality television "participants who present as so comfortable on camera that they behave in ways that suggest they forget about the cameras, or who are so overcome by emotion that they cannot contain themselves despite the cameras" (Dubrofsky 2016, p. 664). As effective as Trump's reality-show campaign was at generating unpaid advertising, his use of Twitter had the added benefit of allowing him to circumvent the mainstream media altogether (Johnson 2017, p. xiv).

The use of social media platforms in political campaigning did not begin, of course, with the 2016 election cycle. To date:

> The research literature on social media and election campaigns can be divided into three main strands . . . the *historical development* of digital campaigns . . . the level of *professionalisation* of campaigns . . . [and] the level of *interaction with voters* in social media campaigns.
>
> (Enli 2017, p. 51)

Scholarship in these areas relating to the 2016 presidential campaign has stressed three points. With respect to historical development, Twitter played a more significant role in Trump's campaign than in Clinton's or in any previous presidential campaign. Specifically, as mentioned previously, it was central to Trump's ability to generate free media. According to Peter Francia (2017), "Twitter delivered the equivalent of $402 million in free attention for Trump as compared to $166 million for Clinton based on MediaQuant estimates" (p. 9). With regard to the professionalization of digital campaigns, Trump actually benefitted from a lack of professionalization. As Gunn Enli (2017) explains: "Compared to the Clinton campaign's innovative use of digital media, extensive use of staffers, and the democratic party's expertise, the Trump campaign seemed pretty amateurish . . . [which likely strengthened] the image of [the] candidate as authentic" (p. 58). On the matter of interaction with voters, research indicates that Trump's use of Twitter favored passive consumption:

> American voters who used social media to actively participate in politics by posting their own thoughts and sharing or commenting on social media were actually more likely to not support Trump as a candidate. Yet, those who were more passive receivers of political information via social media were more likely (by 1.26 times) to support Trump as their preferred candidate.
> (Groshek and Koc-Michalska 2017, pp. 1397–1399)

Importantly, such passivity bolstered Russian attempts to influence the 2016 US presidential election. Post-election data and analysis highlight four main conclusions regarding Russia's election activities:

1. *Russia actively and aggressively sought to interfere in the election.* US and British intelligence agencies have conclusively determined that Russia, under President Vladimir Putin's leadership, engaged in an organized cyberterrorist efforts to influence the 2016 US presidential election. These efforts functioned on multiple, intersecting fronts, including the theft and strategic release of Democratic emails, attacks on voter registration lists and voting machines, and a highly coordinated campaign of disruption and disinformation on social media (McCarthy 2017). Commenting on the latter front, Narayanan et al. (2018) observed:

   > In its review of the recent US elections, Twitter found that more than 50,000 automated accounts were linked to Russia. Facebook has revealed that content from the Russian Internet Research Agency has reached 126 million US citizens before the 2016 presidential election.
   >
   > (p. 1)

2. *Russia's cyberterrorist attack on the election was orchestrated to aid Trump and to damage Clinton.* One avenue of attack involved hacking the emails of the Democratic National Committee (DNC) and slowly and strategically leaking those emails to cause maximum harm to Clinton. A second avenue of attack involved amplifying the polarized political environment in the US by "stoking disagreement and division around a plethora of controversial topics such as immigration and Islamophobia" (McCarthy 2017). This included Russian trolls posing as black activists affiliated with the Black Lives Matter movement in an effort to inflame racial tensions (Parnham 2017; O'Sullivan and Byers 2017; Clifton 2018; Stewart et al., 2018). A third avenue of attack entailed posting pro-Trump propaganda online. According to Badawy et al. (2018), "There were about 4 times as many Russian Trolls posting conservative views as liberal ones, [and] the former produced almost 20 times more content." Of these propaganda efforts, the creation and circulation of fake news was among the most effective.

3. *Russian efforts to influence the election in favor of Trump relied heavily on fake news.* Not only did fake news heavily favor Donald Trump over Hillary Clinton (Allcott and Gentzkow 2017), but it was also more widely shared by conservatives and more likely to be believed by them (Ehrenreich 2017). As Emily Stewart (2018) reports, "Conservatives were much more likely than liberals to retweet Russian trolls in the 2016 election," retweeting them roughly 31 times more often. In fact, according to Badawy et al. (2018), "Although an ideologically broad swath of Twitter users were exposed to Russian trolls in the period leading up to the 2016 US presidential election, it was mainly conservatives who helped amplify their message." The role of fake news in the election was further heightened by the fact that fake news spreads faster and more frequently than truth online. In fact, according to one study, "It took the truth about six times as long as falsehood to reach 1500 people. . . . [and] falsehoods were 70% more likely to be retweeted than the truth" (Vosoughi et al. 2018, p. 1148).

4. *Russia's cyberterrorist efforts to swing the election in Trump's favor were successful.* Given the centrality of Twitter to Trump's campaign, the targeted efforts of Russia to use Twitter and other social media platforms to interfere in the election, the evidence that those efforts were especially effective among conservatives and Trump followers, and the exceedingly close nature of the election, there is no question that Russia influenced the outcome of the 2016 presidential election. This marks the first time in US history

that a hostile foreign government successfully altered the result of a US presidential election. While research plainly supports the conclusion that Russia swung the election in Trump's favor, it is not yet clear whether the Trump campaign actively conspired with Russia to subvert a free and fair election. What we know with certitude is that millions of Americans unwittingly participated in a Russian cyberterrorist campaign to elect Donald J. Trump president of the United States.

Presidential Rhetoric

According to Theodore Otto Windt, Jr. (1986),

> A President has three general areas of power available to him [sic]. He has constitutional and statutory power granted by the Constitution or conferred by law. He has political power as head of his party. And he has the power of public opinion.
>
> (p. 102)

For many decades, Windt further observes, presidential studies concentrated almost exclusively on the first two forms of power. That began to change, however, with the publication of Richard Neustadt's 1960 book *Presidential Power: The Politics of Leadership*, in which Neustadt argues that "Presidential *power* is the power to persuade" (p. 11). Since then, there has been a growing interest in presidential rhetoric and, more specifically, the president's ability to influence public opinion through what Theodore Roosevelt dubbed the "bully pulpit." For Jeffrey K. Tulis (1987), growing interest in the "rhetorical presidency" is not so much the product of historical oversight as it is a transformation of the presidency itself, one that occurred under the presidencies of Roosevelt and Wilson.

According to Tulis (1987), the rhetorical practices of the presidency shifted dramatically from the nineteenth century to the twentieth century, a shift that caused the "dilemmas of modern governance" (p. 17). To understand those dilemmas requires an historical consideration of the Constitution and the intention of the Framers who, distrustful of popular appeals, established the separation of powers and independence of the executive branch specifically to guard against demagoguery. According to Ceasar et al. (1981), "the Founders discouraged any idea that the President should serve as a leader of the people who would stir mass opinion by rhetoric" (pp. 161–162). Rather, in their view, the president was a constitutional officer who performed tasks specific to the executive branch; these tasks emphasized communication with Congress more so than with the people. Presidents throughout the nineteenth century largely adhered to this norm. According to Tulis (1987), the Founders believed that presidential rhetoric should be "*public* (available to all) but not thereby *popular* (fashioned for all)" (46). Theodore Roosevelt began to alter this normative expectation through his speaking campaigns, such as his effort to advance national regulation of the railroads. But this shift, which Tulis argues constituted a "basic change in the understanding of the place of the presidency in the political order" (p. 13), was more fully realized by Woodrow Wilson, who regarded the separation of powers as a constitutional defect, and sought to bypass Congress by speaking directly to the American people. This reversal of the founding perspective is dangerous, according to Tulis, because it removes constitutional checks on popular leadership. The deleterious result of this shift is the heightened possibility of populist demagoguery that, in turn, threatens reasoned, deliberative processes.

Like Tulis, other scholars of presidential rhetoric have explored the changing role of presidential leadership and discourse in the modern era. Scholars such as Roderick P. Hart (1984) and Elvin T. Lim (2018), for instance, have both made key contribution to the understanding of modern presidential rhetoric. In his 1984 book *Verbal Style and the Presidency: A Computer-Based Analysis*, Hart created DICTION, a computer-aided text-analysis program that allowed him to examine five linguistic variable across many contexts: (a) *optimism*—language that is positive or supportive; (b) *activity*—language that stresses change, movement, and implementation; (c) *realism*—language that is tangible and immediate; (d) *commonality*—language that emphasizes shared values; and (e) *certainty*—language that is resolute and totalistic. Though this approach has yet to be applied to Trump's presidential rhetoric, one might reasonably expect—in light of its aggrieved tone—a lower score in optimism, and—in light of its populist authoritarianism—a higher score in activity and certainty.

The political scientist Elvin T. Lim (2018) has also studied long-term trends in presidential rhetoric. In his 2018 book *The Anti-Intellectual Presidency: The Decline of Presidential Rhetoric from George Washington to George W. Bush*, Lim found that over time presidential rhetoric has become more anti-intellectual, more abstract, more assertive, more democratic, and more conversational. The trend toward anti-intellectualism is based on the average readability level of presidential discourse, which according to Lim declined from a college-graduate level throughout the eighteen and nineteenth centuries to an eighth-grade level in the 1980s; it also became simpler during that same period with average sentence length dropping from 50 words per sentence to fewer than 20. In a recent study of the readability and simplicity of Trump's rhetoric, Orly Kayam (2018) found that it conforms to the trend of anti-intellectualism identified by Lim. In fact, Kayam concluded that Trump's discourse averages a fourth- to fifth-grade level, the lowest of any candidate during the 2016 campaign by an average of four to five grade levels and the lowest of any president in history (p. 86).

Another prominent and productive line of research into presidential rhetoric concerns matters of genre. Since presidents are "expected to honor certain rhetorical traditions when they address the public" (Louden 2008, p. 634), many scholars have sought to identify the various occasions or categories of presidential rhetoric (inaugural address, State of the Union speech, farewell address, war rhetoric, etc.) and the shared traits of those occasions. Commenting on the benefits of this type of scholarship in 1978, Karlyn Kohrs Campbell and Kathleen Hall Jamieson wrote in *Form and Genre*:

> The critic who classifies a rhetorical artifact as generically akin to a class of similar artifacts has identified an undercurrent of history rather than comprehended an act isolated in time. . . . One may argue that recurrence arises out of comparable rhetorical situations, out of the influence of conventions on the response of rhetors, out of universal and cultural archetypes ingrained in human consciousness, out of fundamental human needs, or out of a finite number of rhetorical options or commonplaces. Whatever the explanation, the existence of the recurrent provides insight into the human condition.
>
> (pp. 26–27)

Campbell and Jamieson followed this work in 1990 with *Deeds Done in Words: Presidential Rhetoric and the Genres of Governance*, in which they argued that rhetors do not simply respond to situational constraints, but that they actively construct situations and audiences. "Skillful presidents not only adapt to their audiences," they write, "they engage in transforming those who hear them into the audiences they desire" (p. 5). In keeping with this perspective, much of the scholarship in this tradition examines how presidents construct a sense of the national character while in office.

Given Trump's relatively short time in office at this point (about two years), research on Trump's rhetoric from the perspective of genre is just emerging. What the nascent scholarship overwhelmingly stresses, however, is Trump's penchant for social and political norm breaking and an utter disregard for democratic institutions. Kathleen Hall Jamieson and Doron Taussig (2017), for instance, observe that President's Trump's "rhetorical signature"—his distinguishing mode of expression—reflects "spontaneity laced with Manichean, evidence-flouting, accountability-dodging, and institution-disdaining claims" (p. 620). Joshua Gunn (2018) concurs, suggesting that Trump's rhetoric is best classified as "political perversion," a genre of discourse that features "recurrent disavowal" (p. 163). "As a genre," he elaborates, "perversion ceaselessly forges and reinscribes an identification that disavowals established order" (p. 174). The appeal of this genre, as with all genres of discourse, is primarily affective; it repeatedly stages repudiation, but it does so in a manner that signals acknowledgement (avowal) of the very thing it repudiates. This is why we claimed in the preface "that one of the most reliable predictors of truth in the contemporary political landscape is that the president has asserted its opposite." President Trump's rhetoric repeatedly affirms the opposite of what is often painfully obvious (for instance, "I'm the least racist person you know"), a fact that forces him to defend his outrageous statements with so-called "alternative facts."

One final avenue of research into presidential rhetoric that has received considerable scholarly attention is the role of media. Presidents obviously rely on modern media, especially television, to speak to various constituencies and the American public. Moreover, the actions of presidents—no matter how trivial—are regarded as newsworthy and widely reported on in the press. Therefore, any attempt to understand presidential rhetoric must take into account both the means by which presidents communicate with the public and the nature of their relationship with the press. Based on Trump's time in office thus far, it is possible to draw four conclusions about Trump's use of media and his relationship with the press:

1.　*Trump is exceedingly skilled at manipulating the news cycle, often driving the news narrative and, thus, setting the public agenda.* The political antics, e.g., building suspense for upcoming episodes, making outrageous and offensive claims, insulting and demeaning others, and tweeting at irregular times, that made candidate Trump irresistible to the press during the 2016 presidential campaign have continued and even intensified since the election. From staged dramas announcing his Supreme Court nominees to high-profile summits with Kim Jong-un and Vladimir Putin, Trump powerfully influences what the press is talking about if not always how. But his most obvious strategy for impacting the news of the day has been his active Twitterfeed. As Julian Zelizer (2018) wrote, "The national conversation has been shaped through his Twitter stream, his tweets quickly making their way onto the television networks."

2. *Trump and Fox News have formed a dangerous and closed feedback loop.* No one other than himself has ever accused President Trump of being a "genius," as most of his ideas are, in fact, not his. The positions and policies that Trump spouts endlessly on Twitter often originate with political commentators (not be confused with journalists) on Fox News, and, in particular, with Sean Hannity, who regularly advises the president in private (Grynbaum 2018). As has been well documented, for instance, Trump routinely tweets ideas and opinions he has just seen on Fox News entertainment programs like *Fox & Friends*. As Zelizer (2018) notes, Trump "depends on television—namely the Fox News network—as a key source for his daily script." Subsequently, those same programs favorably discuss the president's tweets, resulting in a closed feedback loop. "*Fox News*," elaborates Robert Reich, "is no longer intermediating between the public and Trump. *Fox News* is Trump. Trump takes many of his lies from *Fox News*, and *Fox News* amplifies Trump's lies" (2018). When the programming on Fox News is not feeding the president his opinions, it "often carries his speeches live and in their entirety" (Bauder 2018), giving the president billions of dollars in free advertising.

3. *Trump has attacked a free and independent press in Orwellian fashion.* Historically, fake news referred to propaganda or deliberate disinformation, but following his election Trump regularly began to describe any unfavorable press coverage of him as "fake news." As negative coverage of his presidency increased, he escalated his attacks on mainstream news outlets like CNN, MSNBC, the *New York Times*, and the *Washington Post*, referring to them on Twitter and at rallies as the "enemy of the people." Then, on July 24, 2018, at a speech in Kansas City to the Veterans of Foreign Wars annual convention, Trump said, "Stick with us. Don't believe the crap you see from these people, the fake news. . . . What you're seeing and what you're reading is not what's happening" (Remarks by President Trump 2018). The statement echoes a line from George Orwell's (1949) dystopian novel *1984* in which a totalitarian state manipulates the public by policing independent thought: "The party told you to reject the evidence of your

eyes and ears. It was their final, most essential command" (p. 91). Trump's continual effort to discredit news that he does not like ranks among his most chilling rhetoric, especially in light of how successful it has been.

4. *Trump's rhetorical attacks on the press have been effective with his base.* Recent polls suggest that Trump's followers trust him more (by a significant margin) than they trust the news media (Kay 2017). They trust him more despite the fact that he lies more frequently and more outrageously than any US president in history, and despite the fact that he owes his election to the cyberterrorist efforts of a hostile foreign power. As an authoritarian leader whose popularity depends upon a cult of personality, Trump's followers accept his pronouncements as the "gospel truth" (Kellner, 2017, p. 44), and chief among his pronouncements is to not trust their own eyes and ears. Trump's anti-democratic attacks on the press have benefitted from three interrelated factors. First, he partially circumvents the traditional news media by tweeting directly with his followers. Second, online networks like Twitter are especially well suited for transmitting affect (Hillis et al. 2015; Papacharissi 2015), in this case white rage, which resonated with the anger and racism of his followers. Third, Fox News, the most popular 24-hour cable news network, "immunize[s] its viewers from evidence that contradicts their reality . . . It's steady stream of messages affirms its audience's worldview and enables it to dismiss other media outlets that present evidence of wrongdoing by Trump and his associates" (Chang 2018).

Why Trump's Discourse Matters

There is an old saying that "actions speak louder than words." This saying is rooted in a naïve and mistaken view of language, one that contributes to the popular misperception that rhetoric is "empty." Far from being empty or inconsequential, however, rhetoric is material and meaningful. Rhetoric *is* action. It actively defines situations and people, which influences not only how persons respond to those situations and people, but also limits what persons are even able to conceive of as possible responses. It actively alters persons' ideas, values, and beliefs, contributing to and constraining what and how they think. It actively generates emotion and affect, altering how people feel and behave. It actively mobilizes people to action or inaction in all contexts all of the time. What people say does more than simply express who they are and what they are feeling and thinking, though it does those

Chang, A. 2018. Trump needs his alternate reality to survive—and he knows it. *Vox* [online]. Available at: www.vox.com/2018/7/25/17611854/trump-alternate-reality-survival [Accessed 20 August 2018].

Cillizza, C. 2017a. Donald Trump has made conspiracy theories great again. *CNN.com* [online]. Available at: http://edition.cnn.com/2017/07/03/politics/trump-conspiracy-theories/index.html [Accessed 20 August 2018].

Cillizza, C. 2017b. Donald Trump just keeps lying. *CNN.com* [online]. Available at: http://edition.cnn.com/2017/08/03/politics/donald-trump-mexico-boy-scouts-lies/index.html [Accessed 20 August 2018].

Cillizza, C. 2017c. Trump isn't going quiet on Russia. *CNN.com* [online]. Available at: http://edition.cnn.com/2017/08/04/politics/trump-russia/index.html [Accessed 20 August 2018].

Clifton, D. 2018. Russian trolls stoked anger over Black Lives Matter more than was previously known. *Mother Jones* [online]. Available at: www.motherjones.com/politics/2018/01/russian-trolls-hyped-anger-over-black-lives-matter-more-than-previously-known/ [Accessed 20 August 2018].

Coates, T. 2017. The first white president. *The Atlantic* [online]. Available at: www.theatlantic.com/magazine/archive/2017/10/the-first-white-president-ta-nehisi-coates/537909/ [Accessed 20 August 2018].

Cohen, C. 2017. Donald Trump sexism tracker: Every offensive comment in one place. *The Telegraph* [online]. Available at: www.telegraph.co.uk/women/politics/donald-trump-sexism-tracker-every-offensive-comment-in-one-place/ [Accessed 20 August 2018].

Davis, J.H., Sullivan, E., and Benner, K. 2018. Trump tells Sessions to 'stop this rigged witch hunt right now.' *New York Times* [online]. Available at: www.nytimes.com/2018/08/01/us/politics/trump-sessions-russia-investigation.html [Accessed 20 August 2018].

Dubrofsky, R.E. 2016. Authentic Trump: Yearning for civility. *Television & New Media*, 17(7), pp. 663–666.

Ehrenreich, J. 2017. Why are conservatives more susceptible to believing lies? *Slate* [online]. Available at: www.slate.com/articles/health_and_science/science/2017/11/why_conservatives_are_more_susceptible_to_believing_in_lies.html [Accessed 17 August 2018].

Enli, G. 2017. Twitter as arena for the authentic outsider: Exploring the social media campaigns of Trump and Clinton in the 2016 US presidential election. *European Journal of Communication*, 32(1), pp. 50–61.

Ewen, S. 1996. *All consuming images: The politics of style in contemporary culture*. New York: Basic.

Farrell, D.M. 1996. Campaign strategies and tactics. In: L. LeDuc, R. Niemi, and P. Norris, eds., *Comparing democracies: Elections and voting in global perspective*. Thousand Oaks, CA: Sage, pp. 160–183.

Francia, P.L. 2017. Free media and Twitter in the 2016 presidential election: The unconventional campaign of Donald Trump. *Social Science Computer Review*, 36(4), pp. 440–455.

Garrett, M. 2017. Trump changes stance on several campaign promises early in presidency. *CBS News* [online]. Available at: www.cbsnews.com/news/

trump-changes-stance-on-several-campaign-promises-early-in-presidency/ [Accessed 20 August 2018].

Gartner, J. 2017. Donald Trump's malignant narcissism is toxic: Psychologist. *USA Today* [online]. Available at: www.usatoday.com/story/opinion/ 2017/05/04/trump-malignant-narcissistic-disorder-psychiatry-column/ 101243584/ [Accessed 20 August 2018].

Green, E. 2017. It was cultural anxiety that drove white, working class voters to Trump. *The Atlantic* [online]. Available at: www.theatlantic.com/politics/ archive/2017/05/white-working-class-trump-cultural-anxiety/525771/ [Accessed 20 August 2018].

Groshek, J. and Koc-Michalska, K. 2017. Helping populism win? Social media use, filter bubbles, and support for populist presidential candidates in the 2016 US election campaign. *Information, Communication & Society*, 20(9), pp. 1389–1407.

Grynbaum, M.M. 2018. Fox News once gave Trump a perch. Now it's his bullhorn. *New York Times* [online]. Available at: www.nytimes.com/2018/07/01/ business/media/fox-news-trump-bill-shine.html [Accessed 20 August 2018].

Gunn, J. 2018. On political perversion. *Rhetoric Society Quarterly*, 48(2), pp. 161–186.

Hariman, R. 1995. *Political style: The artistry of power*. Chicago: University of Chicago Press.

Harris, M. 2015. It really can happen here: The novel that foreshadowed Donald Trump's authoritarian appeal. *Salon* [online]. Available at: www.salon. com/2015/09/29/it_really_can_happen_here_the_novel_that_foreshadowed_ donald_trumps_authoritarian_appeal/ [Accessed 20 August 2018].

Hart, R. 1984. *Verbal style and the presidency: A computer-based analysis*. Orlando: Academic Press.

Hearn, A. 2016. Trump's 'reality' hustle. *Television & New Media*, 17(7), pp. 656–659.

Heclo, H. 2000. Campaigning and governing: A conspectus. In: N.J. Ornstein and T.E. Mann, eds., *The permanent campaign and its future*. Washington, D.C.: American Enterprise Institute and the Brookings Institute. pp. 1–37.

Hillis, K., Paasonen, S., and Petit, M. 2015. *Networked affect*. Cambridge, MA: The MIT Press.

Hollihan, T.A. 2009. *Uncivil wars: Political campaigns in a media age*, 2nd ed. Boston: Bedford.

Jamieson, K.H. 1996. *Packaging the presidency: A history and criticism of presidential campaign advertising*, 3rd ed. New York: Oxford University Press.

Jamieson, K.H. and Taussig, D. 2017. Disruption, demonization, deliverance, and norm destruction: The rhetorical signature of Donald J. Trump. *Political Science Quarterly*, 132(4), pp. 619–650.

Johnson, D.W. and Brown, L.B., eds. 2018. *Campaigning for president 2016: Strategy and tactics*. New York: Routledge.

Kay, K. 2017. Why Trump's supporters will never abandon him. *BBC News* [online]. Available at: www.bbc.com/news/world-us-canada-41028733 [Accessed 20 August 2018].

Kayam, O. 2018. The readability and simplicity of Donald Trump's language. *Critical Studies Review*, 16(1), pp. 73–88.

Kellner, D. 2017. *American horror show: Election 2016 and the ascent of Donald J. Trump*. Boston: Sense Publishers.

Kessler, G., Lee, M., and Kelly, M. 2017. President Trump's first six months: The fact-check tally. *The Washington Post* [online]. Available at: www.washingtonpost.com/news/fact-checker/wp/2017/07/20/president-trumps-first-six-months-the-fact-check-tally/?utm_term=.11d1a68144da [Accessed 20 August 2018].

Kirk, C., Philbrick, I.P., and Roth, G. 2016. 230 things Donald Trump has said and done that make him unfit to be president. *Slate* [online]. Available at: www.slate.com/articles/news_and_politics/cover_story/2016/07/donald_trump_is_unfit_to_be_president_here_are_141_reasons_why.html [Accessed 20 August 2018].

Kruse, M. and Gee, T. 2016. The 37 fatal gaffes that didn't kill Donald Trump. *Politico* [online]. Available at: www.politico.com/magazine/story/2016/09/trump-biggest-fatal-gaffes-mistakes-offensive-214289 [Accessed 20 August 2018].

Louden, A. 2008. Presidential communication. In: L.L. Kaid and C. Holtz-Bacha, eds. *Encyclopedia of political communication, vol. 2*. Thousand Oaks, CA: Sage, pp. 631–639.

Langer, G. 2017. President Trump at 100 days: No honeymoon, but no regrets. *ABC News* [online]. Available at: http://abcnews.go.com/Politics/president-trump-100-days-honeymoon-regrets-poll/story?id=46943338 [Accessed 20 August 2018].

LeTourneau, N. 2017. Hillary was right. Trump is temperamentally unfit to be president. *Washington Monthly* [online]. Available at: http://washingtonmonthly.com/2017/04/20/hillary-was-right-trump-is-temperamentally-unfit-to-be-president/ [Accessed 20 August 2018].

Lewis, S. 1935. *It can't happen here*. New York: Doubleday, Doran & Co.

Lim, E.T. 2018. *The anti-intellectual presidency: The decline of presidential rhetoric from George Washington to George W. Bush*. Oxford: Oxford University Press.

Los Angeles Times. 2017. Our dishonest president. *Los Angeles Times* [online]. Available at: www.latimes.com/projects/la-ed-our-dishonest-president/ [Accessed 20 August 2018].

Lowry, R. 2017. Trump's normality problem. *Politico* [online]. Available at: www.politico.com/magazine/story/2017/04/trumps-bare-knuckles-approach-comes-with-a-price-214990 [Accessed 20 August 2018].

Lynch, C. 2017. Can we lose the liberal jingoism? Loose talk about "treason" is only harming the resistance. *Salon* [online]. Available at: www.salon.com/2017/06/24/can-we-lose-the-liberal-jingoism-loose-talk-about-treason-is-only-harming-the-resistance/ [Accessed 20 August 2018].

Marcotte, A. 2017a. Yes, it's really this simple: Donald Trump is a cranky, obsessive racist. *Salon* [online]. Available at www.salon.com/2017/09/09/

yes-its-really-this-simple-donald-trump-is-a-cranky-obsessive-racist/ [Accessed 20 August 2018].

Marcotte, A. 2017b. Team Trump's pileup of fake conspiracies: Best possible way to conceal the real one." *Salon* [online]. Available at: www.salon.com/2017/08/02/trumps-pileup-of-fake-conspiracies-best-possible-way-to-conceal-the-real-one/ [Accessed 20 August 2018].

Massumi, B. 2015. *Politics of affect*. Malden, MA: Polity Press.

Mauger, C. n.d. TV Ad watch: Donald Trump aired about $654k in ads in Michigan. *Michigan Campaign Finance Network* [online]. Available at: http://mcfn.org/node/292/tv-ad-watch-donald-trump-aired-about-654k-in-ads-in-michigan [Accessed 20 August 2018].

McCarthy, T. 2017. How Russia used social media to divide Americans. *Guardian* [online]. Available at: www.theguardian.com/us-news/2017/oct/14/russia-us-politics-social-media-facebook [Accessed 17 August 2018].

McElwee, S. and McDaniel, J. 2017. Economic anxiety didn't make people vote Trump, racism did. *The Nation* [online]. Available at: www.thenation.com/article/economic-anxiety-didnt-make-people-vote-trump-racism-did/ [Accessed 20 August 2018].

Milbank, D. 2015. Donald Trump is a bigot and a racist. *The Washington Post* [online]. Available at: www.washingtonpost.com/opinions/donald-trump-is-a-bigot-and-a-racist/2015/12/01/a2a47b96-9872-11e5-8917-653b65c809eb_story.html?utm_term=.788257191acf [Accessed 20 August 2018].

Milbank, D. 2016. Trump reverts to his xenophobic self. *The Washington Post* [online]. Available at: www.washingtonpost.com/opinions/trump-reverts-to-his-xenophobic-self/2016/08/31/03a0ed6c-6fc8-11e6-9705-23e51a2f424d_story.html?utm_term=.a98b5f627ec3 [Accessed 20 August 2018].

Moffitt, B. 2016. *The global rise of populism: Performance, political style, and representation*. Stanford, CA: Stanford University Press.

Morris, A. 2017. Why Trump is not mentally fit to be president. *RollingStone* [online]. Available at: www.rollingstone.com/politics/features/trump-and-the-pathology-of-narcissism-w474896 [Accessed 20 August 2018].

Moye, D. 2017. Here's a list of every single Trump lie since he took office. *HuffPost* [online]. Available at: www.huffingtonpost.com/entry/every-single-trump-lie_us_594d85cce4b02734df2a7bc1 [Accessed 20 August 2018].

Narayanan, V. et al. 2018. Polarization, partisanship and junk news consumption over social media in the US. *Comprop Data Memo*, 1, pp. 1–9.

Neustadt, R.E. 1960. *Presidential power: The politics of leadership*. New York: Wiley & Sons.

O'Connor, L. 2017. Here are 16 examples of Donald Trump being racist. *HuffPost* [online]. Available at: www.huffingtonpost.com/entry/president-donald-trump-racist-examples_us_584f2ccae4b0bd9c3dfe5566 [Accessed 20 August 2018].

Orwell. G. 1949. *1984*. New York: New American Library.

O'Sullivan, D. and Byers, D. 2017. Exclusive: Fake black activist accounts linked to Russian government. *CNN.com* [online]. Available at: https://money.cnn.com/2017/09/28/media/blacktivist-russia-facebook-twitter/index.html [Accessed 20 August 2018].

Ott, B.L. 2017. Affect. In: J.F. Nussbaum, ed., *Oxford research encyclopedia of communication*. New York: Oxford University Press.

Ouellette, L. 2016. The Trump show. *Television & New Media*, 17(7), pp. 647–650.

Papacharissi, Z. 2015. *Affective publics: Sentiment, technology, and politics*. Oxford: Oxford University Press.

Parnham, J. 2017. Russians posing as black activists on Facebook is more than. *Wired* [online]. Available at: www.wired.com/story/russian-black-activist-facebook-accounts/ [Accessed 20 August 2018].

Parry-Giles, S. et al. 2017. 2016 presidential advertising focused on character attacks, not policy. *Huffpost* [online]. Available at: www.huffington-post.com/the-conversation-us/2016-presidential-adverti_b_13090306.html [Accessed 20 August 2018].

Reich, R. 2018. Robert Reich: Donald Trump is a liar. Don't let him get away with it. *Newsweek* [online]. Available at: www.newsweek.com/robert-reich-donald-trump-liar-dont-let-him-get-away-it-opinion-1019084 [Accessed 20 August 2018].

Remarks by President Trump at the Veterans of Foreign Wars of the United States National Convention, Kansas City, MO, 2018. *Whitehouse.org* [online]. Available at: www.whitehouse.gov/briefings-statements/remarks-president-trump-veterans-foreign-wars-united-states-national-convention-kansas-city-mo/ [Accessed 20 August 2018].

Robbins, M. 2017. Of course Trump defended O'Reilly. *CNN.com* [online]. Available at: http://edition.cnn.com/2017/04/05/opinions/trump-defended-bill-oreilly-robbins/index.html [Accessed 20 August 2018].

Scalia, C.J. 2016. Donald Trump is a pragmatist, too. *The Washington Post*, 29, May, p. B01.

Schmitt, M. 2016. What Trump exposed about the G.O. P. *New York Times* [online]. Available at: www.nytimes.com/2016/11/11/opinion/identity-over-ideology.html?mcubz=2 [Accessed 20 August 2018].

Schneider, C. 2017. The conservative guide to impeaching Trump. *USA Today* [online]. Available at: www.usatoday.com/story/opinion/2017/03/17/conservative-guide-impeaching-trump-christian-schneider-column/99256148/ [Accessed 20 August 2018].

Shapiro, B. 2016. Is Donald Trump a pragmatist? *National Review* [online]. Available at: www.nationalreview.com/article/442221/donald-trump-pragmatist-not-conservative [Accessed 20 August 2018].

Spinoza, B. 1992. *Ethics: Treatise on the emendation of the intellect and selected letters*, trans. S. Shirley. Indianapolis, IN: Hackett Publishing Company.

Stein, J. 2017. Study: Hillary Clinton's T. ads were almost entirely policy-free. *Vox* [online]. Available at: www.vox.com/policy-and-politics/2017/3/8/14848636/hillary-clinton-tv-ads [Accessed 20 August 2018].

Stewart, E. 2018. Study: conservatives amplified Russian trolls 30 times more often than liberals in 2016. *Vox* [online]. Available at: www.vox.com/policy-and-politics/2018/2/24/17047880/conservatives-amplified-russian-trolls-more-often-than-liberals [Accessed 17 August 2018].

Stewart, J. 2017. The 1935 novel that predicted the rise of Donald Trump. *Guardian* [online]. Available at: www.theguardian.com/us-news/shortcuts/2016/oct/09/it-cant-happen-here-1935-novel-sinclair-lewis-predicted-rise-donald-trump [Accessed 20 August 2018].

Stewart, L., Arif, A., and Starbird, K. 2018. Examining trolls and polarization with a retweet network. In: *Proceedings of WSDM workshop on misinformation and misbehavior mining on the web (MIS2)*. New York: ACM.

Strömbäck, J. and Kiousus, S. 2014. Strategic political communication in election campaigns. In: C. Reinemann, ed. *Political communication*. Berlin: Gruyter, pp. 109–128.

Tesfamichael, N. 2017. Trump's job approval remains steady in Pew Survey. *Politico* [online]. Available at: www.politico.com/story/2017/06/20/trump-approval-ratings-pew-239756 [Accessed 20 August 2018].

Trump. D.J. 2018, August 1. Available at: https://twitter.com/realdonaldtrump/status/1024646945640525826 [Accessed 17 August 2018].

Tulis, J. 1987. *The rhetorical presidency*. Princeton, NJ: Princeton University Press.

Vivian, B. 2002. Style, rhetoric, and postmodern culture. *Philosophy and Rhetoric*, 35(3), pp. 223–243.

Vosoughi, S., Roy, D., Aral, S. 2018. The spread of true and false news online. *Science*, 359(6380), pp. 1146–1151.

Winberg, O. 2017. Insult politics: Donald Trump, right-wing populism, and incendiary language. *European Journal of American Studies* [e-journal], 12(2) Available through: Openedition Journals [Accessed 20 August 2018].

Windt Jr., T.O. 1986. Presidential rhetoric: Definition of a field of study. *Presidential Studies Quarterly*, 16(1), pp. 102–116.

Zelizer, J. 2018. Where is Trump's Emmy nomination? *CNN.com* [online]. Available at: www.cnn.com/2018/07/14/opinions/trump-white-house-drama-emmy-nomination-opinion-zelizer/index.html [Accessed 20 August 2018].

2 The Politics of White Rage

Following the 2016 presidential election, many commentators feared that Fox News would be little more than a mouthpiece for President Trump (Sullivan 2017). The reality, however, is substantially more disturbing. Nearly two years into office, it is now clear that Trump is a mouthpiece for Fox News. An avid viewer of conspiracy-themed television programs like *Fox & Friends* and *Hannity*, Trump regularly regurgitates—often in impulsive, ill-conceived, early-morning tweets—the outrageous talking points he encounters on these pseudo-news programs. In fact, Trump clearly trusts Fox TV personalities more than he trusts US intelligence agencies, whom he routinely disagrees with and disparages (Kiely 2017). To the extent that Trump and the White House articulate anything approaching a clear, consistent ideology, which they rarely do, it originates with Fox News, Trump's advisors, or his racists supporters on Reddit. There is, in fact, widespread recognition and agreement that Trump does not subscribe to any political ideology (Bruni 2016; Jones n.d.). As Damon Linker (2016) has pointed out, "Trump has shown no ideological consistency at all—not even for a new kind of ideology." On the contrary, Trump regards himself as highly "flexible,"[1] prides himself on being a "deal-maker" (Thrush and Haberman 2017), and frequently and unabashedly contradicts and reverses himself on matters of policy (Cillizza 2017). As Ana Marie Cox astutely observed, "He's too lazy to have an ideology himself, so he just kind of lets other people think it up for him" (cited in Legum 2016).

Absent a core set of values or beliefs, Trump's rhetorical appeal and subsequent political success is, as we suggested in Chapter 1, best viewed through the lens of style. The style that he performs is rooted in pervasive sentiments (anxiety and fear) about race that are shared by "primarily white, working class Christians who believe the U.S. has been in decline for years" (Keller 2016). This segment of the American electorate cling to "the belief that the changes molding modern America have marginalized them economically, demographically, and culturally" (Brownstein 2016). They share, as Daniel Cox observes, "a visceral feeling of being left behind" and, as Cornell Belcher notes, "a cultural nostalgia, for when white male culture [was] most dominant" (quoted in Brownstein 2016).

As Chauncey Devega (2016) elaborates in *Salon*: "Trump's base of white working-class authoritarians is scared of what they view as a 'new' America, one in which they believe that the psychological and material wages of Whiteness will not be as great." While "Trump is not necessarily the prime instigator or cause of those fears," he was, as Devega (2016) observes, "the most adept at manipulating them."

This chapter seeks to explain Trump's manipulations of the fear and anxiety surrounding the social decentering of white privilege[2] and hegemonic masculinity through reference to the concept of white rage. Toward that end, this chapter proceeds in two parts. First, we discuss how white rage functions aesthetically and affectively; in short, we demonstrate that white rage is the basis of Donald Trump's rhetorical style and, thus, widely evident in his general manner of communicating. Second, we analyze Trump's performative expression of white rage. Attending to public video of his speeches, we show how his speaking style—including nonverbal, paraverbal (intonation, vocal tone, and the like), and linguistic elements—reproduces and enacts the affective aesthetics of white rage, which in turn stokes racial animus and provides substantial comfort to those for whom Trump's message resonates.

Before proceeding with our analysis, however, a few words regarding the somewhat unique nature of our approach are in order. Because style is enacted through embodied performance and because we do not have direct access to President Trump, we combine careful rhetorical analysis of publically available recordings of his speeches with extensively collected media and press coverage. Our analysis of the videos of Trump's speaking allow us to engage Trump's embodied performance of already existing affective and aesthetic structures of white rage. In this study, we bring our full, sensing bodies to the rhetorical task as we explore the sounds and the visuality of white rage along with its linguistic structures. Our exhaustive engagement with popular press coverage of Trump's performances provides anecdotal evidence for how bodies other than our own have and continue to react to Trump. While this approach is not without its limitations, it allows us to (re)construct Trump's performative style as it is experienced by a large portion of the populace, namely in a mediated fashion. But it also means that the analysis we undertake explicitly blends criticism with political commentary as data for our argument. This approach is consistent with our assertion below that affect is not individual but social, and that affect functions in a specific moment but is structured through historical and cultural practices. We operationalize this social, cultural, and historical understanding of affect and aesthetics by bringing our own two bodies to the speeches and weaving our responses with the published traces of others. We hope that readers find the atypical character of our critical intervention to be a meaningful and productive one.

The Rhetorical Appeal of White Rage

Affect

In the previous chapter, we defined affect as precognitive and autonomic energy that circulates and engages bodies. We also noted that these (largely) precognitive responses should not be imagined to be without history or devoid of mediation. Derek Hook (2006) explains that while affect may well register in the moment as pre-discursive, the affective structures themselves are partially and in some cases largely built through discursive interactions. Hook (2006) writes that, "The underlying grid of such [affective] associations is not itself 'pre-discursive,' but is instead necessarily supplied by a social sphere of political values and norms, by discourse" (p. 219). As Hook suggests, our embodied memories that make possible affects like revulsion, eroticism, or the abject are already social, are structured discursively, and are historically and culturally specific. It is crucial to this project to hold in combination these two dimensions of affect. In short, we regard affect as, at the same time, precognitive in its energy *and* social, historical, political, and discursive in its structure and in its consequence. Racism, in particular, should be understood as at least a partially affective structure in which the cognitive and symbolic nature of racism is discursively and iteratively performed and over time becomes part of many of our bodies' sensate structures (Hook 2006). Racism is a materially consequential affective structure. It structures bodily affective engagements, it structures affective energy in public spheres, and it has powerful and deeply damaging material consequences.

Aesthetics

We also noted in the Chapter 1 that the formal, stylistic, tropological, and primarily non-symbolic elements of rhetoric's aesthetics are organized energies that perform and trigger the bodies' affective capacities (Whitson and Poulakos 1993). Words can appeal to the body and can be structured rhetorically for the purpose of this embodied aesthetic appeal. Likewise, the non-symbolic parts of rhetorical performances—the grain of the voice, the order of the words and their rhythms, the form of the gestures—are organized invitations to precognitive affect. The voice's grain and the gesture's form are, at least partially, the body's performance of affect. And if affect is the excitation of that which arises when bodies interact, then these nonverbal and paraverbal performances invite other bodies' affects in the affective expression. In this formulation, aesthetics and affect, while not the same thing, are co-constitutive. The body's affect materializes in discourse through rhythms, vocal patterns, gestures, and turns of phrase. Likewise, and at the same time, rhythms, vocal patterns, gestures, and turns of phrase affects the body. Thus, we maintain that *affective aesthetics is a dynamic, inter-relational force produced between and among bodies, all of which bear traces of lived experience, cultural structures, and historical forms.*

White Rage

Affective aesthetics links the sensual, immediate, and prediscursive responses of bodies to specific environmental energies with historically situated discursive processes and practices. Acknowledging this linkage aids us in evaluating the political and rhetorical consequentiality of affective aesthetics. As we argued in the previous chapter, this conception honors Gilles Deleuze and Felix Guattari's radical idea that instead of ideology or structures of meaning and rationality, there are events whose power is registered affectively (Deleuze and Guattari 1988 cited in Massumi 2015, p. 91). Such a view is particularly well suited to aid in understanding and assessing an emergent politically charged affective aesthetics, especially as embodied and enacted by someone who has been described as a non-ideological pragmatist and "ideology-free populist" (Scalia 2016; Schmitt 2016; Schneider 2017). To reiterate our argument in Chapter 1, claiming that affect is non-ideological does not deny the importance of power. Rather, affect and power are intimately interwoven, for power already mounts particular affective structures even as affective events perform and materialize power relations (Massumi 2015, p. 19).

The affective aesthetics of white rage works to trigger racist rage in individuals and to do so at a nonrational, embodied level. Whiteness—and the racism that it expresses, and which supports it—is old and powerful. It has a deep history and a full range of affective and aesthetic entailments. Whiteness is commonly understood to be an invisible or nearly unrecognizable political and cultural center around which all other US identities circulate. As Thomas Nakayama and Robert K. Krizek (1995) argue, whiteness is a position without position, a center without center. Non-linear and constantly seeking to hide itself, whiteness nonetheless organizes everyday life in the US. "'White' is a relatively uncharted territory," Nakayama and Krizek (1995) write,

> that has remained invisible as it continues to influence the identity of those both within and without its domain. It affects the everyday fabric of our lives but resists, sometimes violently, any extensive characterization that would allow for the mapping of its contours. It wields power yet endures as a largely unarticulated position.
>
> (p. 291)

While not directly interested in questions of affect, Nakayama and Krizek recognize the affective power of whiteness and resistances to its decenterings. Like affect, whiteness functions invisibly, which is to say precognitively and apparently beyond critical engagement and symbolization. The effort to bring whiteness to the level of awareness, to make the precognitive cognitive or the nonsymbolic symbolic is met with violent resistance—that is to say with nearly inchoate rage.[3]

It is hard to explain this rage with rational or linear reasoning. Indeed, Nakayama and Krizek draw on the non-linearity of Delezuian thought to help explore the slipperiness of whiteness and to call for a critique of whiteness's assemblages. The affective rage at uncovering whiteness's territory depends, we suggest, on the ways race in the US is already an abjected structure. The white rage experienced when whiteness is revealed is the psychic other side of the revulsion and disgust that register racism on the body. Building a sense of self—individually or socially—depends on abjection. We cast from ourselves parts of ourselves and then, when confronted directly with this abjected other we feel horror and revulsion. In the US, race has played this role. Racial others are repulsive remainders of the self; racial otherness is the contingently and constantly abjected. Such revulsion registers on the level of the body and functions prediscursively even though, as we argued above, it is formed and made compelling discursively. Whiteness, then, depends on repelling racial others. In US culture, blackness is the archetypal other, but of course whiteness repels all other forms of racial otherness as Trump's rhetoric demonstrates. There is, undoubtedly, a circularity to this process of creating whiteness through abjection. The other that is abjected must first be created before it can be repulsed. And, yet, the repulsion depends on the affective belief that the racial other preexists the affective abjection (Hook 2006).

The substantial advantage of weaving this affective understanding of race with other more symbolic and cultural understandings of race is that it helps keep the body at the forefront of analysis. Explaining the embodied rage and the felt repulsion of racial others is nearly impossible from a rational or symbolic perspective.[4] Racism certainly appears and is performed in discourse, and yet its powerful force registers in the body as an affect more than an idea. To understand the potency of racism we must explore the affective and aesthetic dimensions of discourse.

White rage is felt in the body, is triggered by aesthetics, and depends on the generations-old affective structures of racism. This rage is the embodied, prediscursive affective response to directly confronting the boundaries between white and non-white. This rage struggles mightily to maintain a white subjectivity that is always already at risk, is always contingent, and always depends on deeply felt rejection of non-white identities. This prediscursive rage—which we must say again is absolutely connected to discourses, histories, and the politics of racism—is at the heart of Trumpian appeals. Deeply historical, the affect of racism is built out of the centuries of slavery, Jim Crow era atrocities, anti-immigrant, and anti-Native American policies and practices. In fact, it is precisely the length and depth of this history and its many, daily performances of hatred that gives this discourse its power at the affective embodied level. And so, while the affect of white rage is felt in very specific moments and by individual bodies, it is a rage that is centuries and generations old. The body that feels the rage may be young, but the rage itself is older than the nation.

There are two powerful advantages to thinking of white rage in terms of aesthetics and affect. First, it allows us to understand the ways that rage registers on the body in a particular moment and cannot be easily mitigated by rational discourse. Rationality and reasoned discourse fail to temper or alleviate white rage because of the ways rage activates prediscursive structures and because these prediscursive structures are embedded in long, deep, tangled, and powerful histories of racial hatred in the US. Second, by theorizing a co-constitutive relationship between the aesthetic dimensions of racist discourse and the affective responses these discourses invite, we can understand Trump's rhetorical performances of white rage as deeply historical and as an expression of US American affective truths. This is precisely why we do not locate Trump as the originator of a white rage as a rhetorical style. His performances are, instead, crystallizations and perfections of already existent structures. Rather than calling an audience into being, Trump's rhetoric performs centuries of masculinist racism. Trump speaks an affective aesthetic that at the same time speaks him. Trump's followers deeply desire the affective aesthetics Trump performs, even as Trump himself is constructed by and through these desires. As he remarked at one rally, "is there anything more fun than a Trump rally?"—a question that acknowledges how audience and speaker excite one other through long-held affective structures (Trump TV Network 2016).

The affective aesthetics of white rage is ideally suited for demagogic rhetoric. Patricia Roberts-Miller, while clearly arguing that we ought not define demagoguery in terms such as "passion, emotionalism, populism, and pandering to crowds" defines demagoguery as political speech that relies on us/them thinking, where policies need not be debated because one is for those things one already believes in and, subsequently, against everything *they* are for. Political decision-making concerns "three stases," Roberts-Miller (2017) writes:

> group identity (who is in the in-group, what signifies out-group membership, and how loyal rhetors are to be in the in-group); need (the terrible things the out-group is doing to us, and/or their very presence); and what level of punishment to enact against the out-group (ranging from the restriction of the out-groups' rights to extermination of the out-group).
>
> (p. 33)

Crucially, like racism and white rage, demagoguery proceeds particular rhetors; it is an already available rhetorical resource individual rhetors may draw on to make their rhetoric. We agree with Roberts-Miller that demagoguery is not confined to the reactionary right or to racists. But we also agree that demagoguery easily aligns with authoritarianism and is a powerful response to fear. "The culture of hatred and fear preexist, and the demagogue uses them" (Roberts-Miller 2005, p. 472). In the next pages, we detail the particular ways Trump takes advantage of both the preexisting structures of demagoguery and those of white rage. Combining these approaches, we explore the ways Trump's rhetoric does the work of demagoguery and does so through the more specific rhetorical style of the affective aesthetics of white rage.

More specifically still, Trump's performance of white rage and bodily responses to the aesthetic expression of it entails two main stylistic dimensions. The first is a brash, unapologetic performance of white privilege, including authoritarian and autocratic action both of which well express white hegemonic masculinity. The second is the performance of indignation at the social decentering of whiteness. Through his embodied performance of these two dimensions, Trump materially induced a range of affective responses in other bodies. For those bodies whose histories and memories resonated with this style, Trump excited them. He excited them to uncritical adulation, to cheers and ovations at his rallies; he excited them to expressions of racial animus on social media, in their homes, and at their workplaces; he excited them to a visceral loathing of racial otherness, foreigners, and Barack Obama; he excited them to intense hatred of women generally and Hillary Clinton specifically; and he excited them to a distrust of democratic institutions like a free press and independent judiciary. While Donald Trump did not create white rage, he exploited it for personal and political gain. In the remainder of this chapter, we explore the precise ways in which he did so.

Trump's Performance of White Rage

Managerial Style: On Trump's Leadership

Embracing the anti-elitism typical of a populist, Trump campaigned not as a politician, but as a successful business*man* and entrepreneur, repeatedly touting his experience as a tough negotiator and skilled dealmaker. Known for his catch phrase "you're fired," Trump drew on his hyper-aggressive business image to build his political style. During the campaign, Trump promised to bring his you're fired business style to the US government, which he insisted had been horribly mismanaged under Obama. At one point, Trump went so far as to say that Russian President Vladimir Putin was a better leader than US President Barack Obama (Keneally 2016). In fact, Trump regularly infused his political rhetoric with management discourse such as when a woman asked Trump what he would say to Obama. He interrupted her, saying "you're fired," at which point the crowd erupted, their bodies instantaneously responding to a white man putting a black man in his place (World Wide Videos 2016). In light of Trump's campaign rhetoric, which elevated authoritarian image (attack politics) over substance (actual policy), it is worth analyzing Trump's authoritarian style in greater detail.

While demagogic rhetoric can infest all places on the political spectrum, "it most easily aligns with some version of what the linguist George Lakoff has called 'strict father' model and some scholars call authoritarianism" (Roberts-Miller 2017, p. 44).[5] One of Roberts-Miller's important arguments about demagoguery is that it can be just as effective—and prevalent—outside of the political realm. We find demagogic rhetoric in entertainment, in corporations, in efforts to make money. And Trump first realizes the powerful resources demagogic culture allows in his career as a reality TV star and Fox News commentator. In 2012, several years before Trump announced his bid for the presidency, management scholar Andrew DuBrin (2012) noted, "Donald Trump is a power-oriented business leader and celebrity with a brusque and autocratic leadership style" (p. 364). An autocratic leader, elaborated DuBrin (2012), is "A task-oriented leader who retains most of the authority for himself or herself and is not generally concerned with group members' attitudes toward decisions" (p. 363). Trump affirmed his predilection for an autocratic style before and after the election, praising other world leaders who adopt this approach, including Egyptian President Abdel-Fatah el-Sissi, Turkish President Recep Tayyip Erdogan, and Chinese President Xi Jinping (Salama and Pace 2017). As with any leadership style, different leaders enact it differently. So, the particulars of Trump's performance matter. His autocratic style is characterized by three principal traits: (1) unbridled authority, (2) uninhibited intimidation, and (3) unfettered egotism. In short, Trump is controlling, coercive, and conceited, a combination of traits that embody white privilege and hypermasculinity and that were central to the affective appeal of his leadership style among his base.

Authority, of course, describes the degree to which a leader has the power to control resources, make unilateral decisions, and instruct others what to do. The degree to which highly concentrated authority is publicly accepted and acceptable is constrained by an array of social and cultural factors (e.g., race and gender) and legal and political contexts (e.g., democratic vs. non-democratic). Both whiteness and masculinity afforded and continue to afford Trump wide latitude in his authoritarian performance, latitude that would have never been granted to his predecessor or challenger. Imagine, for instance, if President Obama or Secretary Clinton had—referring to the social and economic challenges facing the country—bragged, as Trump did at the Republican National Convention in July, 2016, "I alone can fix it" (CNN 2016a). They would have been labeled "uppity," "arrogant," or far worse, and it would have ended their political careers. In fact, we do not have to imagine this: Secretary Clinton constantly confronted and lost to this very structure.[6]

Trump's performance of authoritarianism benefitted him in two interconnected ways during the campaign. First, it appealed both to far-right-wing conservatives, who tend to prefer authoritarianism (Pettigrew 2017), and to a majority of working-class whites, who polling showed "believed the country needs an authoritarian leader (defined as someone 'who will break the rules because things have gotten so far off track')" (Keller 2016). Second, it allowed Trump to say ("I moved on her like a bitch. . . . And when you're a star, they let you do it. You can do anything. . . . Grab 'em by the pussy. You can do anything") and do (repeatedly interrupt Secretary Clinton during the presidential debates) egregiously misogynistic (and racist) things without alienating his base. To the contrary, the more "out of bounds" Trump's actions, the more degrading his treatment of women (from Carly Fiorina to Megyn Kelly), the more racially charged his campaign rallies, the more denigrating his remarks about "elite" politicians (from Barack Obama to Ted Cruz), the more vicious his rebukes of the "mainstream" media—the more it affectively stoked energy and excitement among his followers.

The appeal of authoritarianism among many white voters was grounded in their belief that "people like them" are worse off today; they sense that they are increasingly socially, politically, and economically decentered and disadvantaged. By a margin of nearly 2 to 1, the white working class believes, "American culture has gotten worse since the 1950s," that "the U.S. is in danger of losing its identity, and . . . [that] America's growing number of immigrants threaten the country's culture" (Green 2017). While Trump's white nationalist, anti-immigrant rhetoric powerfully dovetailed with his no-holds-barred autocratic and authoritarian style that affectively mobilized his supporters. Trump demonstrates a consistent refusal to be constrained, bucking not only social norms, but also—after being elected—the constitutional limits of his authority (Collinson 2017). In his first few days in office, for instance, he issued a racially and religiously charged executive order banning citizens and refugees in six Muslim majority countries from entering the US. When a series of courts ruled that he had exceeded his statutory authority, Trump took the unprecedented step of attacking the judiciary (Liptak 2017).

Trump's attack on the courts, much like his repeated attacks on the press as "fake news," suggest that his chief concern is actually his image as an authority. He believes that his voice is the authoritative voice on all matters and that his decisions must be followed regardless of traditional constraints. Simply put, he will not tolerate anything that makes him look bad or, more importantly, anything that makes him look weak, i.e., feminine. To guard against this, Trump has long insisted that his employees sign non-disclosure agreements (Cook 2016), which prior to him becoming president often included non-disparagement clauses that prevent them from saying anything critical about him. Trump's efforts to manage his image extend well beyond attempts to control what others say, however. After *The New York Times*, *Saturday Night Live*, and other media outlets speculated that chief strategist Steve Bannon was calling the shots in the White House (President Bannon? 2017), Trump quickly sought to reestablish his authority by removing Bannon from the National Security Council (Baker et al. 2017). He also ordered a military strike in Syria, an action some suggested he lacked the legal standing to authorize (Epps 2017), and one which we maintain was a transparent attempt to reassert his masculine authority. In short, Trump's "words and actions have," as Yascha Mounk (2017a, 2017b) explains, "consistently betrayed his authoritarian instincts."

These instincts are buttressed by two additional traits: coercion and conceitedness. By coercion, we mean Trump's willingness to use intimidation and threat, often of lawsuits, to get what he wants. A few of the institutions and individuals Trump has threatened, either as a candidate or president, include the press (both in general and with specific news outlets), the judiciary, any woman who makes allegations of sexual assault against him, GOP senators who have not adequately supported him, members of his own administration who leak to the press, the Department of Justice, former FBI Director James Comey, and special counsel Robert Mueller. While these actions are alarming to many, to Trump followers they demonstrate the president's "toughness." When asked about his firing of James Comey, one supporter admiringly said it showed he's "not afraid to take action" (Trip et al. 2017).

Few consistently repeated moments, both on the campaign trail and after elected, represent this authoritarian coercion as well as the "lock her up" chants. Started during the campaign in response to Trump's badgering about Clinton's emails, the chant became a major theme of the Republican National Convention with the audience regularly interrupting speakers with the chant. The power of these shared commitments has continued into Trump's presidency. On September 22, 2017 in a campaign style rally in Huntsville, Alabama, President Trump riffs on the ways "crooked Hillary" would have taken away rifles if elected. "If crooked Hillary had got elected," he says, "you would not have a Second Amendment, believe me. You would be handing in

The Politics of White Rage 39

your rifles, you would be saying here, here" and he gestures as though handing in his rifle (*Washington Post* 2017).[7] Traversing the stage, he pantomimes handing in rifles to authorities as the audience shouts "lock her up, lock her up." Looking disgusted with having to hand in his guns, his expression turns to pleasure as the audience chants "lock her up." He spreads his arms wide nodding his head as though to say: you and I are one, we agree, we excite each other. Then, shaking his head and shrugging to indicate he would lock her up if he could, if only the bounds of propriety and the law were finally fully loosed, Trump continues to pace the floor then returns to the microphone and says, "You gotta speak to Jeff Sessions about that." His voice drops with masculine force. Together the audience and Trump build an affectively powerful relationship demanding the imprisonment of the un-liked other while coercing Attorney General Sessions to bend to popular will.

In addition to coercion, Trump's authoritarian leadership style reflects an unfettered egotism marked by an inability to admit wrongdoing (Wolson 2017). Trump, for instance, regularly makes fantastical, self-involved claims such as, "I will be the greatest jobs president that God ever created, I tell you that" ("I will be the greatest" 2015). In addition to being delusional, Trump speaks and acts with absolute conviction on all things, even those things that directly contradict his previous statements.[8] In short, Trump *never* admits he is wrong; he demonstrates a total unwillingness to take responsibility for anything, no matter how trivial, if it challenges his delusional image of himself. Trump invariably, then, scapegoats others for his mistakes, poor judgment, and personal inadequacies, errors and shortcomings that are legion.

Consider, for instance, the efforts to separate children from parents of immigrants and refugees at the nation's southern border. While the administration's claims about why they are separating children from parents vary—Attorney General Jeff Sessions using biblical authority (Zauzmer and McMillan 2018), presidential advisor Stephen Miller saying the policy is smart and a good deterrent (Porter 2018), Secretary of Homeland Security Kirstjen Nielsen saying that the administration does not have a policy to separate children from parents (Chappell and Taylor 2018)—Trump has only ever blamed Democrats for the practice. Not once, according to analysis by the *Washington Post*, has he accepted responsibility for the new actions. He has lied repeatedly to deny responsibility for the family separation policy. Those lies always point to Democrats as the author of the critiqued actions (Parker 2018).

Trump's unwillingness to admit any wrong-doing combined with authoritarian coercion also marked his response to the racial violence in Charlottesville, Virginia on August 12, 2017. White nationalists rallied on August 11 and 12 with chants of "blood and soil" as they protested the removal of antebellum, pro-Confederacy statues. Protestors responded to the racist and fascist demonstrators and the confrontation soon turned violent with James Alex driving a car into the middle of the protestors killing Heather Heyer. Trump's first response, coming many hours after the incident, was tepid. He devotes a small portion of an event honoring veterans to a statement about the violence perpetrated by the blood-and-soil activists. At the very beginning of the event, he turns to shake the hands of the veterans who have joined him on stage. When he walks back to the podium, his eyes are down and he uncharacteristically grabs the podium and reads a prepared statement. His vocal tone is even keel with no emotive inflection that creates a mismatch with the strong language; he intones: "we condemn in the strongest possible terms this egregious display of hatred, bigotry, and violence on many sides, on many sides." Trump's delivery of this sentence is crucial to its rhetorical function. Through most of the sentence, his delivery is monotone, his eyes are down avoiding the audience and the camera, and he is clearly reading. As he reads the text, he inserts a long pause between "terms" and "this egregious." He tilts his head as if to read the words correctly and indicating a distance between his body and his mind, between the words he is reading and what he really believes. He marks his resistance to condemning hatred by this pause, this head tilt, this hesitancy. When he arrives at "on many sides," however, his delivery changes. He looks up from his notes, connects with the audience, offers a gesture (removing his right hand from the podium) and his vocal tone acquires energy. In a now familiar delivery style, Trump offers "on many sides, on many sides" in the same mode that he offers so many of his other Trumpian truths (CNN 2017).

In this delivery, Trump's body invites viewers' bodies to sense that the first words are the politically correct statements, the words written by technocrats, by traditional politicians. In the final phrasing, viewers' bodies can see, hear, and feel the real Trump. Suddenly, the affectively authentic speaker equates fascists and racists with the counter-protestors. The power of this maneuver is not produced nor can it be understood through the speech text even as the words already do important affective work. Instead, it is the embodied performance, the delivery of the words that let the world know Trump's soul is with the blood and soil racists.

When, however, he is critiqued for his lackluster condemnation of the right-wing activists and, even more, when he is questioned for his moral equivocation, he does not apologize. He rejects the opportunity to emphasize his refutation of the racist protestors. Instead, he defends and elaborates "on many sides." Angrily, he repudiates the critics and he clarifies through his delivery that he finds the counter-protestors to be more repugnant than the neo-Nazis who organized the march (Merica 2017). Far from apologizing for his inept initial response, he turns the criticism into an opportunity to fully perform white rage. In his performance at the August 15, 2017 press conference at Trump Tower (Global News 2017), he performs his rage, shouting down reporters, gesturing broadly, and speaking without notes. The physical contrast between the initial statement and this performance indicates that the second is the authentic Trump. His embodied anger materialized commitments to the racists in Charlottesville and among his followers. In so doing, he offers an aesthetically and affectively powerful mode for others to join him in rage. He makes public, publicly available, and acceptable this rage.

Trump's authoritarian style—with its controlling and coercive tendencies, and Trumpian delusions—afforded comfort for a set of widely shared fears and anxieties among the white working class.[9] Trump did much more than merely promise to "Make America Great Again" through his rhetoric; he enacted it through his leadership style. Trump embodied the very "greatness" (i.e., authority, power, pride, and confidence) to which his followers feel that they are entitled and to which they feel unduly stripped by foreigners, racial minorities, feminists, and the liberal elite. That Trump had no coherent political ideology or even policy proposals did not matter; they were not voting for a specific plan but a general sensibility, a staged performance of whom they wished to be. Trump's explicit performance of privileged white male rage performed an embodied rhetorical style and at the exact same time appealed affectively to at least some white bodies, to those bodies' memories of a bygone era in which they, too, viscerally enjoyed the unearned assets of such privilege.

Physical Style: On Trump's Embodied Rage

While we have begun to assess the matter of embodiment in the context of Trump's authoritarianism, his physical performance is so important that it demands attention in and of itself. Indeed, a second key dimension of his populist rhetoric is his physical style or general deportment, by which we mean his overall demeanor and associated mannerisms, as well as his appearance, which includes his "spectacularly unusual hairstyle" (Wells 2017), signature orange glow, and attire. Trump's overall demeanor, which like his management style reflects white male privilege, can accurately be summarized as aggressive, angry, and derisive of anyone different from him and those he favors. While this basic demeanor has remained relatively consistent throughout his public life, the rhetorical ends served by that demeanor shifted when he transitioned from candidate Trump to President Trump. During the campaign, Trump positioned himself as a political outsider (and in many ways he was) and, consequently, his brash behavior served a carnivalesque function. After Trump's election, however, that same behavior became a tool of intimidation and coercion. So, while the rhetorical figure that best characterizes Trump's demeanor during the campaign is that of the fool, the rhetorical figure that best captures it after the election is that of the bully.

Trump's embodiment of the fool was central to his material and affective appeal during the campaign. The concept of the fool, as we are using it, derives from the Russian literary scholar Mikhail Bakhtin's (1984) study of medieval carnival. According to Bakhtin, in the medieval era, celebrations such as the "feast of fools" and the "feast of the ass" were opposed to the serious official feasts and elite political ceremonies of the established order and, thus, "marked the suspension of all hierarchical rank, privileges, norms, and prohibitions" (p. 10). They were decidedly populist affairs marked by their own logic, peculiar aesthetic (grotesque realism), and modes of expression (spectacle, parody, and abusive language). The closest thing to medieval carnival in the contemporary context, with the possible exception of professional wrestling events (which, oddly, Trump has also been involved in), is Donald Trump's campaign rallies, unruly affairs that celebrated "the people" by degrading and debasing the political elite.[10]

A central figure in medieval folk culture and carnival is the fool. Fools, writes Bakhtin (1984), exercise the right,

> *not* to understand, the right to confuse, to tease, to hyperbolize life; the right to parody others while talking, the right to not be taken literally, . . . the right to rip off masks, the right to rage at others with a primeval (almost cultic) rage.

(p. 163)

Trump is, by any standard, a fool, a repulsive know-nothing clown who desperately "hopes for mainstream culture's endorsement" (Williams 2015, p. 113). His mocking impersonations of Hillary Clinton and his primary Republican challengers at disorderly, often raucous, campaign events were, to use Bakhtin's (1984) words, "special forms of . . . speech and gesture, frank and free, permitting no distance between those who came in contact with each other and liberating from norms of etiquette and decency imposed at other times" (p. 10).

Trump's crude and indecorous manner, his grandiose and exaggerated mannerisms, capture the aesthetic of grotesque realism, "the lowering of all that is high, spiritual, ideal, abstract . . . to the material level, to the sphere of earth and body" (Bahktin 1984, p. 19). The embodied examples of Trump's foolery are endless. Best known, perhaps, is his mocking of a disabled reporter. In endlessly shared video clips from CNN and other news sources, Trump going into character as the disabled reporter waves his arms uncontrollably though held tight to his body, his voice suddenly an octave higher and stuttering (CNN 2015). Reminiscent of playground behavior or of a poorly conceived comedy routine, Trump equates physical and mental disability. The audience roars with approval as Trump creates a powerfully constituted "us" that relegates any sign of otherness to a deeply despised outside.[11] Trump performs disgust with the other and, as Martha Nussbaum (2010) argues, disgust is one of the most powerful ways of relegating others to non-human status (pp. 13–26).

But Trump performs this foolish disgust again and again; he gets so worked up about the supposed rapists from Mexico infiltrating the nation that spittle gathers on the side of his mouth (C-SPAN 2015). He finds Hillary Clinton so loathsome that he stalks her about the debate stage on October 9, 2016. Constantly peering over her shoulder and menacingly approaching her from behind whenever she was speaking, Trump acted like a WWE wrestler in a suit. He performs for his followers the kind of "creepy" aggression that characterizes misogynistic masculinity. His body is performing the rhetoric, his face enacting masculine rage. He stalks Clinton as though she does not belong on the stage, and as though he wishes to push her off it. In so doing, he invites those already invested in the belief that only men should be president to share his affective response to Clinton. He does not need to speak misogynistic words; his embodied actions are far more powerful. This stalking combines with Trump's dismissal of Megyn Kelly as a menstruating woman and the derision of the *New York Times* reporter and the spittle gathering on the side of the mouth to express and call forth disgust for non-white, non-males, non-able bodied bodies. Trump uses his body to dismiss the bodies of all those not like him, and he uses his body to trigger a similar dismissal by his followers. Not only does Trump perform and invite gendered and racialized disgust, but his actions can speak to anyone whose disgust with others has been ridiculed. This is exactly why so many Trump followers proudly took on the moniker of "deplorable." The powerfully felt dismissal in the term deplorable returns in Trump inspired, embodied disgust with all who are different.

Grotesque realism, elaborates Bakhtin (1984), is all about "the lower stratum of the body, the life of the belly and the reproductive organs" (p. 21). This aesthetic was evident, as Kira Hall et al. (2016) observe, in "Trump's expressions of disgust regarding the embodiment of others, whether in reaction to Megyn Kelly's menstruation, Hillary Clinton's toilet behaviors, or Marco Rubio's sweating" (p. 82), as well as his claim during a Republican presidential debate that his penis is not undersized ("I assure you there's no problem *down there*"). But the grotesque is also evident in Trump's physicality with his gauche manner. In contrast to former President Obama, whose defined jaw, sculpted body, well-groomed appearance, and graceful movement reflect a classical aesthetic, Trump's lumbering movement constitutes "a refusal of the dominant corporeal aesthetic" (Bennett 2016) and viscerally concretizes his populist and anti-elite sentiment.

The populist appeal of Trump's countless grotesqueries—his gestural excesses, bodily parodies, contorted facial expressions—was reinforced by his attire. From his ill-fitting suit jackets and trousers to his brightly colored, scotch taped, too-long ties, which sought to assure us of his masculine, phallic power, Trump gave the appearance of the common man. This appearance was literally capped off by a red, white, or occasionally camouflaged "baseball cap"—sometimes called a "trucker's cap"—embroidered in all capital letters, as if shouting in those rare moments when he was not, "MAKE AMERICA GREAT AGAIN." Looking at and listening to Trump, his followers participated in a shared fantasy, an alternate image of themselves, one in which they, like Trump, were an American success story. Trump *is*, in fact, an American success story, not in the ways his supporters believe, a so-called "self-made man," but the benefactor of tremendous wealth and privilege, a con-man who built a real estate empire by cheating and deceiving others. That Trump's followers did not and do not see him as a con-man, that contrary to all available evidence they see him as their champion, is a product of the affective resonance between his grotesque style and their own embodied anger and frustration at a political elite they believe has abandoned them.

Whereas candidate Trump leveraged his body and bodily movements to transgress all manner of social and political norms, and to play the disruptive role of the fool, that option was no longer available to him after the election, for he then held the very position of authority he had sought to uncrown. Consequently, Trump went from playing the role of a bull in a china shop to playing the role of a bully. While "Trump's bullying style" (Prose 2017) is evident in many of his mannerisms, perhaps none more obviously than his trademark handshake, an aggressive grab and yank that aims to assert his alpha male status (quoted in Hosie 2017a). Trump often utilizes an overly aggressive handshake style when meeting and interacting with other powerful men such as when he greeted newly elected French President Emmanuel Macron at the NATO summit in Brussels.[12] We say men here because Trump does not regard any woman—even a world leader—as his equal and, therefore, does not see female leaders as a threat to his masculinity. Nor was Trump's white-knuckle exchange with Macron the only action in which "The American president came off looking like a bully" at the NATO summit (Kirschbaum 2017). His most unabashed display of bullying behavior occurred when he shoved aside the Prime Minister of Montenegro, Duško Marković, to reposition himself at the forefront of a group of world leaders (Schmidt 2018). Though Marković (2017) brushed off the incident, calling it "a harmless situation," Trump's supporters overwhelmingly and excitedly approved of it. One Trump supporter told CNN, "It's great. We love it. We're America" (Moos 2017). Trump's followers appreciate his bullying behavior because it affirms their sense of "American" entitlement, which is simply code for white privilege and hegemonic masculinity that they feel have been lost.

Linguistic Style: On Trump's Discourse

Thus far, we have examined two key aesthetic dimensions of Trump's populist rhetoric: his autocratic style, which provides affective comfort to white working-class voters who feel besieged by decades of alienating social, economic, and political changes that they associate with minorities and immigrants; and his carnivalesque and bullying physical style, which affectively resonates with their anger at the established political elite for the neoliberal policies that they believe led to the aforementioned cultural shifts. In this, the final section of analysis, we explore Donald Trump's linguistic style, which bridges his unapologetic performance of white male privilege with anger at the social decentering of such privilege. This occurs, we argue, through a linguistic style that is equal parts hyperbolic, narcissistic, and demagogic. This typology draws upon prior research conducted by Peter Levine (2016), who has characterized Trump's speech as paratactic,

Gary C. Woodward (2017), who has labeled it self-referential, hyperbolic, needy, and scapegoating, and Sara Ahmadian et al. (2017), who have found Trump's communication style to be defined by grandiosity, informality, and dynamism.

Analyzing President Trump's linguistic style involves looking not so much at *what* he says (at least not primarily so), as *how* he says it. Hence, the first stylistic trait, hyperbole or overstatement, is not about the fact that Trump says outrageous things, but that he says nearly everything outrageously. Regardless of topic or context, Trump speaks in exaggerations. Such exaggeration is evident in his claims to know "more about ISIS than the generals do" and to know "more about renewables than any human being on Earth" (Blake 2016). As David Nakamura (2017) notes, "It's a style that worked successfully for Trump during the campaign, when he spoke to voter anxieties, in often apocalyptic terms." Lacking any sense of nuance, humility, or restraint, Trump expresses whatever he is talking about in the most dramatic and stark terms. Despite the obvious dangers hyperbolic speech poses for political diplomacy and foreign relations, Trump's supporters appreciate his lack of subtlety, which they regard as more authentic than the carefully measured statements of political elites.

In addition to hyperbole, Trump's linguistic style is characterized by narcissism. The president likes to talk about himself and his accomplishments, which given his proclivity for hyperbole often results in stunningly self-aggrandizing claims. This includes estimations of his intellect ("I think [I] would qualify as not smart, but genius . . . and a very stable genius at that" (Diaz 2018)), linguistic abilities ("I know words, I know the best words" (Trump, 'I have the best words,' 2017)), attractiveness ("It's very hard for them to attack me on looks, because I'm so good looking" (Donald Trump on Megan Kelly 2015)), humility ("I think I am actually humble. I think I'm much more humble than you would understand"(Cillizza 2016)), respect for women ("There's nobody who respects women more than I do" (*Today Show* 2016)), and social contributions ("I was the one that really broke the glass ceiling on behalf of women, more than anybody in the construction industry" (Haberman 2016)). As these examples suggest, Trump "bends reality to fulfill whatever fantasy about power, wealth, beauty, etc. he maintains" (Hosie 2014). But the fact that he exhibits no self-questioning is appealing to his supporters, many of whom feel powerless. Trump, in contrast with many of us who consistently doubt our ability, appears "to have none of the insecurities his followers are trying to escape. He is the mirror they look into and wish to see themselves" (Shantz 2017).

The third and final trait of Trump's linguistic style is demagoguery.[13] If demagoguery, as Patricia Roberts-Miller (2005) suggests, "is polarizing propaganda that motivates members of an ingroup to hate and scapegoat some outgroup(s), largely by promising certainty, stability, and what Erich Fromm famously called 'an escape from freedom'" (p. 462) then Trump surely partakes of and performs demagoguery, and his discourse illustrates it (Singer 2015).[14] Throughout the 2016 presidential campaign, Trump—despite his exceptional wealth—repeatedly portrayed himself as a champion of the white working class. At the Republican National Convention, for instance, he pledged to defend "the laid-off factory workers and the communities crushed by our horrible and unfair trade deals," adding that, "these are the forgotten men and women of our country. . . . People who work hard but no longer have a voice. I am your voice" (CNN 2016b). As important as what Trump said was the way he said it, speaking in simple, declarative sentences, and using "a blue-collar accent" and his wearing of his "Make America Great Again" trucker hat (Oprea 2016).[15] Simply put, Trump's voters believed he represented their interests because he spoke in their manner.

Affective identification is powerful rhetorically because it sounds true and feels true; affective affiliation is often produced not by argumentative care but by drawing on a wellspring of cultural speech codes Gerry Philipsen (1986, pp. 257–258) has taught us to identify. These speech codes can create a groundwork for demagoguery when they appeal first and foremost to identity and are used to create us and them distinctions that rely on pervasive stereotypes dehumanizing one or more other. As we have argued throughout, these divisions do not arise in a moment, they are not produced by Trump, and they do not function primarily cognitively. Instead, the othering divisions are old, they are woven into the fabric of culture and the culture's bodies, and the symbolization and enactment of these divisions work viscerally. They are affective energies that motivate bodies beyond and before reason. Writing in *The New York Times*, Alexander Burns (2016) notes:

> On a visceral level, he grasped . . . the raw frustration of blue-collar and middle-class white voters who rallied to his candidacy with decisive force. Mr. Trump rallied them less with policy promises than with gut-level pronouncements—against foreign trade, foreign wars and foreign workers.

Trump's visceral connection to white working-class voters was aided by his use of hyperbolic rejections of others. Joe Romm (2016) explains:

> A key purpose of hyperbole is to express the emotion of anger . . . When Trump makes wildly over-the-top claims—he's going to build a wall and make Mexico pay for it—it . . . persuades them [his followers] precisely because it is hyperbolic nonsense. They are angry, and he's showing that he is angry too—which is vastly more effective.

This hyperbole is an excellent vehicle for expressing anger and for building affective commitments to identity.

Hyperbole is also an effective tool to convey fear of scapegoated others. Trump's fear-mongering rhetoric was an essential feature of his campaign. From the first moment when he announced his candidacy in Trump Tower ("When Mexico sends its people, they're not sending their best. . . . They're sending people that have lots of problems, and they're bringing those problems with us. They're bringing drugs. They're bringing crime. They're rapists" (PBS News Hour 2015)) to his inaugural address ("But for too many of our citizens, a different reality exists . . . the crime and gangs and drugs that have stolen too many lives and robbed our country of so much unrealized potential" (NBC News 2017)) to his comments on a European tour in early July, 2018 ("I just think it [immigration] is changing the culture, I think it is a very negative thing for Europe. I know it is politically not necessarily correct to say that, but I will say it and I will say it loud" (Collinson 2018)), Trump repeatedly stoked racial fears. Again and again, Trump asserted that immigrants, inner-city citizens, and non-white people are destroying—indeed, have destroyed—the nation. The presence of these people, he continues to assert, is cause for deeply felt fear and profoundly sensed loss.

This is the affective terrain of demagoguery. Demagoguery as performed by Trump and nearly every other demagogue, creates a fearsome battle between the good but outnumbered us against a ravaging and bestial them. As Roberts-Miller (2005) writes, "Reactionary demagogues posit a time when identities and roles were stable and when there was perfect agreement. This Edenic stability was destroyed by the outgroup" (p. 473). But this desire for an idealized past and a fear of the present is sensible—that is experienced via the senses. It responds nearly perfectly to the complexity of democracy in the contemporary world. We are asked to make decisions in a world of powerful complexity. We know that our decisions could be wrong, that our way forward may be deeply uncomfortable. We are, in short, afraid of freedom. Drawing on Eric Fromm, Roberts-Miller (2005) writes, "the human possibility of making a decision always involves the equally human possibility of making a mistake—it is the opportunity and responsibility of freedom" (p. 465). But this freedom is frightening, and many people look for a way to escape freedom.

And so, Trump's racist, anti-immigrant discourse throughout the campaign drew on deep and deeply effective tropes which affectively resonated with conservative white working-class voters, who were "angry, afraid and motivated by racial animus, white racial resentment and nativism" (Devega 2016). Trump's rhetoric was appealing both because it emotionally mirrored the anger of his followers and because it directly challenged what they see as an overly PC (politically correct) culture. Trump's willingness to openly say racist and sexist things (he said in Europe about his anti-immigrant statements, "I know it is politically not necessarily correct to say that, but I will say it and I will say it loud"), along with his willingness to attack politicians and the so-called "liberal" media in the most malicious and venomous ways won over voters who were tired of being told what they can and cannot say. As one Trump supporter told the BBC: "I backed Trump from the beginning. Because he calls things out. . . . Donald Trump is not politically correct, and I love that about him" (Election 2016 2016). In fact, post-election polling suggests that one of biggest predictors of voting for Trump "was the rejection of political correctness" (Hutson 2017). While the content of Trump's discourse mattered, his hyperbolic, narcissistic, and demagogic linguistic style was crucial to his affective appeal and, consequently, to his political success.

Implications and Conclusion

We are not the first to point to the racist, misogynistic, authoritarian, and hyperbolic language of Donald Trump. As we have shown through this chapter, many popular press writers and a growing number of academic authors have noted these characteristics. Here we have tried to make two important links. First, we have placed Trump's particular performances within the historical and cultural context of the affective aesthetics of white rage. Just as Patricia Roberts-Miller suggests that as demagoguery preexists and enables the demagogue, so too do the structures of the affective aesthetics of white rage preexist and enable Donald Trump the white racist. Our formulation weaves together an understanding that white rage is centuries old and absolutely located in this present place and time. We argued that white rage is productively understood as affectively powerful and triggered by aesthetics or style. Because white rage often functions on an affective register, attention to texts alone and without attention to form, style, and embodied performance will miss most of the suasory power of the expression of white rage.

In the second part of this chapter, we performed an analysis of Trump's rhetoric, paying particular attention to his affective and embodied performance of white rage. We suggested that this rage is communicated along trajectories familiar to those who have studied demagoguery. The performative style relies on authoritarian white masculinity performed through embodied and linguistic expressions of rage. Trump regularly mocks and expresses disgust with the bodies of others, and he aggressively stalks his opponents. Linguistically, he lies with abandon, refuses to back down when he is caught in prevarications, and adds linguistic fuel to any fire his racist and misogynistic language produces. And, like all rhetors drawing on demagogic culture, he reduces all political debates to issues of identity which rely on and reinforce us/them polarities.

In short, his words neither do their rhetorical work logically nor do they function primarily—or even partially—in the realm of denotative meaning. Instead, the speaking voice and gesticulating body reiterate and reproduce and are produced by affective and aesthetic structures. If ever it seemed true that language speaks the subject, so it is in this instance. White rage is always already powerfully present in US American discourse. We have seen it again and again over the last decades across politicians on both the left and the right. Bill Clinton's war on welfare depended on this white rage just as much as George W. Bush's post-9/11 wars required this rage. Trump, then, is merely the most recent and compelling voice of this rage. As we discuss in the next chapter, Trump's rhetorical performance of white rage is heightened by the truncated and seemingly impersonal form of Twitter.

Notes

1. In Trump's words, "I like to think of myself as a very flexible person. I don't have one specific way, and if the world changes, I go the same way. I don't change—well, I do change. And I am flexible" (Schulberg et al. 2017).
2. By white male privilege, we mean the unearned assets that accrue from simply being white and male. As white males, we too benefit from such privilege. For instance, we can write an essay highlighting the racist and sexist character of Trump's rhetoric largely without fear of violence being visited upon our bodies or having our argument challenged or dismissed because of our bodies.

3. Carol Anderson (2016) offers a powerful historical analysis of US American white rage. She demonstrates that at every turn in US history where blacks or other people of color stake a larger claim to promises of freedom, white rage creates a powerful and lasting backlash such that many if not all of the gains are erased.

4. Hook (2006) writes, "Discourse as such, in the regularity of its categories, in the surety of its reiterated demarcations, is an ally in the attempt to fend off and objectify the abject even though such efforts never prove completely effective. This is why discursive forms of engagement are both absolutely crucial to the analysis of racism but also in and of themselves inadequate to the task" (p. 223).

5. Much of what we find in Trump's rhetoric enacts Roberts-Miller's understanding of demagogic rhetoric. Her wonderful pocket book *Demagoguery and Democracy* names many of the rhetorical patterns we are exploring here. As she writes, however, we need to study particular instances of demagoguery. We are adding a detailed analysis of affect through a broader understand of aesthetics to Roberts-Miller's understanding of demagoguery.

6. See Karrin Vasby Anderson's (2017) work on Hillary Clinton and gender, and presidential politics more broadly.

7. For the full speech, see Trump TV Network (2017).

8. Trump "state[s] his position of the moment (whatever it is) with absolute conviction. (When he adopts a different position the next day, he invariably states *that* with just as much certainty and assurance)" (Linker 2016).

9. As Trudy Rubin (2016) observes, "In their anger at a system that appears broken, many Americans embrace[d] Trump's autocratic values."

10. It is fitting that Trump has been inducted into the WWE Hall of Fame (Donald Trump 2018).

11. Crucially, Trump performs this clown-like stunt as a distraction regarding his debunked claim on the campaign trail that he saw thousands of Muslims celebrating the 9/11 attacks. This is a classic example of demagoguery where genuine concerns are dismissed without engagement, nearly always through some form of us/them discourse.

12. See, for example, the comparison between the handshake between Trump and Macron after Macron greeted many other NATO leaders in Brussels before greeting Trump and then the handshake Trump and Macron shared not long after. In the first, Trump pulls Macron hand so hard, that Macron appears to stumble, reaching up to Trump with his right hand to stabilize himself. In the second, Trump tries to let go before Macron will let him (Macron and Trump's two tense handshake battle 2018).

13. For a more extended analysis of Trump's demagoguery, see Paul Elliott Johnson (2017).

14. Discussions of demagoguery are nearly as old as the nation. See, for example, James Fenimore Cooper (1838) and Michael Singer (2015).

15. Communication and rhetoric has a long interest in understanding the cultural viability of specific speech patterns. Analyzing a speech Daley performed at a city council meeting, Philipsen (1986) notes that the speech was deemed nearly unintelligible by many. But it well conformed to Teamsterville speech patterns and served as a powerfully affective speech to that audience. Like the speech (and delivery) patterns we are analyzing, Teamsterville speech is rooted in time and place, and the speakers enunciate already available cultural forms.

References

Ahmadian, S., Azarshanhi, S., and Paulhus, D.L. 2017. Explaining Donald Trump via communication style: Grandiosity, informality, and dynamism. *Personality and Individual Differences*, 107(1), pp. 49–53.

Anderson, C. 2016. *White rage: The unspoken truth of our racial divide*. New York: Bloomsbury.

Anderson, K.V. 2017. Every woman is the wrong woman: The female presidential paradox. *Women's Studies in Communication*, 40(2), pp. 312–135.

Baker, P., Haberman, M., and Thrush, G. 2017. Trump removes Stephen Bannon from National Security Council post. *New York Times*. Available at: www.nytimes.com/2017/04/05/us/politics/national-security-council-stephen-bannon.html [Accessed August 20, 2018].

Bakhtin, M. 1981. Forms of time and of the chronotypes in the novel. In: M. Bakhtin, ed. *The dialogic imagination: Four essays*. Translated by C. Emerson and M. Holquist. Austin: University of Texas Press.

Bakhtin, M. 1984. *Rabelais and his world*, translated by H. Iswolsky. Bloomington: Indian University Press.

Election 2016: Trump voters on why they backed him. 2016. *BBC News* [online]. Available at: www.bbc.com/news/election-us-2016-36253275 [Accessed August 20, 2018].

Bennett, B. 2016. Trump's body. *The Sociological Review* [online]. Available at: www.thesociologicalreview.com/blog/trump-s-body.html [Accessed August 20, 2018].

Blake, A. 2016. 19 things Donald Trump knows better than anyone else, according to Donald Trump. *The Washington Post* [online]. Available at: www.washingtonpost.com/news/the-fix/wp/2016/10/04/17-issues-that-donald-trump-knows-better-than-anyone-else-according-to-donald-trump/?utm_term=.8a0560820c96 [Accessed August 20, 2018].

Brownstein, R. 2016. Trump's rhetoric of white nostalgia. *The Atlantic* [online]. Available at: www.theatlantic.com/politics/archive/2016/06/trumps-rhetoric-of-white-nostalgia/485192/ [Accessed August 20, 2018].

Bruni, F. 2016. Donald Trump's ideology of applause. *New York Times* [online]. Available at: www.nytimes.com/2016/09/11/opinion/sunday/donald-trumps-ideology-of-applause.html [Accessed August 20, 2018].

Burns, A. 2016. Donald Trump rode to power in the role of the common man. *New York Times* [online]. Available at: www.nytimes.com/2016/11/09/us/politics/donald-trump-wins.html [Accessed August 20, 2018].

C-SPAN. 2015. Donald Trump presidential campaign announcement full speech (C-SPAN) [video online]. Available at: www.youtube.com/watch?v=apjNfkysjbM [Accessed August 20, 2018].

Chappell, B. and Taylor, J. 2018. Defiant homeland security secretary defends family separations. *NPR* [online]. Available at: www.npr.org/2018/06/18/620972542/we-do-not-have-a-policy-of-separating-families-dhs-secretary-nielsen-says [Accessed August 20, 2018].

Cillizza, C. 2016. Donald Trump's interview with '60 minutes' was eye-opening. Also, Mike Pence was there. *The Washington Post* [online]. Available at: www.

washingtonpost.com/news/the-fix/wp/2016/07/18/donald-trump-is-way-more-humble-than-you-could-possibly-understand/?utm_term=.e0de35ba1f4e [Accessed July 22 2018]

Cillizza, C. 2017. Here's an easy way to understand all of President Trump's recent flip flops. *CNN.com* [online]. Available at: edition.cnn.com/2017/04/13/politics/trump-flip-flop-russia-china/index.html [Accessed August 20, 2018].

CNN, 2015. Trump mocks reporter with disability [video online]. Available at: www.youtube.com/watch?v=PX9reO3QnUA [Accessed July 5 2018].

CNN, 2016a. Donald Trump's entire republican convention speech [video online]. Available at:www.youtube.com/watch?v=Fs0pZ_GrTy8 [Accessed August 20, 2018]

CNN, 2016b. Donald Trump, GOP nomination acceptance speech [video online] Available at: www.youtube.com/watch?v=Fs0pZ_GrTy8 [Accessed July 10 2018].

CNN, 2017. Trump addresses Charlottesville clashes (full) [video online]. Available at: www.youtube.com/watch?v=CMQWJDVg8PA [Accessed August 20, 2018]

Collinson, S. 2017. Trump tests the limits of presidential power. *CNN.com* [online]. Available at: edition.cnn.com/2017/07/21/politics/trump-no-limits-president/index.html [Accessed August 20, 2018].

Collinson, S. 2018. Trump: Immigration is 'changing the culture' of Europe. *CNN.com* [online]. Available at:www.cnn.com/2018/07/13/politics/trump-europe-immigration/index.html [Accessed July 26, 2018].

Cook, N. 2016. Trump transition team members sign non-disclosure agreements. *Politico* [online]. Available at: www.politico.com/blogs/donald-trump-administration/2016/12/non-disclosure-agreements-232275 [Accessed August 20, 2018].

Cooper, J.F. 1838. *The American democrat: Or, hints on the social and civic relations of the United States of America.* Cooperstown: H. & E. Phinney.

Devega, C. 2016. Donald Trump's rageful white cult: Race, fear and the GOP front-runner's slick manipulations. *Salon* [online]. Available at: www.salon.com/2016/02/22/donald_trumps_rageful_white_cult_race_fear_and_the_gop_front_runners_slick_manipulations/ [Accessed August 20, 2018].

Diaz, D. 2018. Trump: I'm a 'very stable genius.' *CNN.com* [online]. Available at: www.cnn.com/2018/01/06/politics/donald-trump-white-house-fitness-very-stable-genius/index.html [Accessed July 22, 2018].

Donald Trump, 2018. *World Wrestling Federation* [online]. Available at: www.wwe.com/superstars/donald-trump [Accessed July 5, 2018].

Donald Trump on Megyn Kelly: 'What I said was appropriate.' 2015. *Meet the Press* [online]. Available at: www.nbcnews.com/meet-the-press/trump-what-i-said-was-appropriate-n406661 [Accessed July 22 2018].

DuBrin, A.J. 2012. *Essentials of management*, 9th ed. Mason: South-Western.

Epps, G. 2017. Trump's unlawful attack in Syria, *The Atlantic* [online]. Available at: www.theatlantic.com/politics/archive/2017/04/trumps-unlawful-attack-in-syria/522432/ [Accessed August 20, 2018].

Green, E. 2017. It was cultural anxiety that drove white, working class voters to Trump. *The Atlantic* [online]. Available at: www.theatlantic.com/politics/archive/2017/05/white-working-class-trump-cultural-anxiety/525771/ [Accessed August 20, 2018].

Global News, 2017. Donald Trump's off-the-rails full news conference on Charlottesville response [video online]. Available at: www.youtube.com/watch?v=Ix3764QIBIc [Accessed July 20, 2018].

Haberman, M. 2016. Donald Trump says he broke glass ceiling for women in construction industry. *New York Times* [online]. Available at: www.nytimes.com/2016/06/07/us/politics/trump-fox-news.html [Accessed July 22, 2018].

Hall, K., Goldstein, D., and Ingram, M.B. 2016. The hands of Donald Trump: Entertainment, gesture, spectacle. *HAU: Journal of Ethnographic Theory*, 6(7), pp. 71–100.

Hook. D. 2006. 'Pre-discursive' racism. *Journal of Community & Applied Social Psychology*, 16(3), pp. 207–232.

Hosie, R. 2017a. Donald Trump's handshake: The real meaning explained by body language expert. *Independent* [online]. Available at: www.independent.co.uk/life-style/donald-trump-handshake-meaning-justin-trudeau-shinzo-abe-explanation-body-language-expert-darren-a7579541.html [Accessed August 20, 2018].

Hosie, R. 2017b. 'Malignant narcissism': Donald Trump displays classic traits of mental illness, claim psychologists. *Independent* [online]. Available at: www.independent.co.uk/life-style/health-and-families/donald-trump-mental-illness-narcisissm-us-president-psychologists-inauguration-crowd-size-paranoia-a7552661.html [Accessed August 20, 2018].

Hutson, M. 2017. Why liberals aren't as tolerant as they think. *Politico* [online]. Available at: www.politico.com/magazine/story/2017/05/09/why-liberals-arent-as-tolerant-as-they-think-215114 [Accessed August 20, 2018].

I will be the greatest jobs president god ever created, 2015. *Guardian* [online]. Available at: www.theguardian.com/us-news/video/2015/jun/16/donald-trump-us-president-republicans-video [Accessed, July 22 2018].

Johnson, P.E. 2017. The art of masculine victimhood: Donald Trump's demagoguery. *Women's Studies in Communication*, 40(3), pp. 229–250.

Jones, S. n.d. Donald Trump has no strategy, no beliefs, and no principles. *New Republic* [online]. Available at: newrepublic.com/minutes/141930/donald-trump-no-strategy-no-beliefs-no-principles [Accessed August 20, 2018].

Keller, J. 2016. How the Trump campaign exposed America's sleeping authoritarianism. *Pacific Standard* [online]. Available at: psmag.com/news/how-the-trump-campaign-exposed-americas-sleeping-authoritarianism [Accessed August 20, 2018].

Keneally, M. 2016. Trump says Putin better leader than Obama in military town hall. abcnews.go.com [online]. Available at: abcnews.go.com/Politics/trump-putin-leader-obama-military-town-hall/story?id=41936057 [Accessed August 20, 2018].

Kiely, E. 2017. *Trump and intelligence community. FactCheck.Org* [online]. Available at: www.factcheck.org/2017/01/trump-and-intelligence-community/ [Accessed August 20, 2018].

Kirschbaum, E. 2017. Europe's reaction to the Trump style ranges from envy to 'you tiny, tiny, tiny little man.' *Los Angeles Times* [online]. Available at: www.latimes.com/world/europe/la-fg-trump-europe-impressions-20170526-story.html [Accessed August 20, 2018].

Legum, G. 2016. Donald Trump's lazy, slipshod transition: No ideology, only cynicism and corruption. *Salon* [online]. Available at: www.salon.com/2016/12/09/donald-trumps-lazy-slipshod-transition-no-ideology-only-cynicism-and-corruption/ [Accessed August 20, 2018].

Levine, P. 2016. Trump's rhetorical style and deliberation. *Peter Levine: A Blog for Civic Renewal* [online]. Available at: peterlevine.ws/?p=17752 [Accessed August 20, 2018].

Linker, D. 2016. Donald Trump's post-ideological authoritarianism. *The Week* [online]. Available at: theweek.com/articles/625893/donald-trumps-postideological-authoritarianism [Accessed August 20, 2018].

Liptak, A. 2017. Trump loses travel ban ruling in appeals court. *New York Times* [online]. Available at: www.nytimes.com/2017/06/12/us/politics/trump-travel-ban-court-of-appeals.html [Accessed August 20, 2018].

Macron and Trump's two tense handshake battle. 2018. *Guardian* [online]. Available at: www.theguardian.com/us-news/video/2017/may/25/macron-trump-handshake-battle-video [Accessed July 9, 2018].

Marković, D. 2017. 'Harmless situation' that doesn't affect our friendship. *Time.com* [online]. Available at: time.com/4797972/dusko-markovic-montenegro-nato-donald-trump/ [Accessed August 20, 2018].

Massumi, B. 2015. *Politics of affect*. Malden: Polity Press.

Merica, D. 2017. Trump says both sides to blame amid Charlottesville backlash. *CNN.com* [online]. Available at: www.cnn.com/2017/08/15/politics/trump-charlottesville-delay/index.html [Accessed July 22 2018].

Moos, J. 2017. Trump voters love the shove. *CNN.com* [online]. Available at: edition.cnn.com/videos/politics/2017/06/20/donald-trump-love-the-shove-moos-pkg-erin.cnn [Accessed August 20, 2018].

Mounk, Y. 2017a. Authoritarian by instinct. *Slate* [online]. Available at: www.slate.com/articles/news_and_politics/the_good_fight/2017/07/trump_is_an_authoritarian_by_instinct_not_ideology.html [Accessed August 20, 2018].

Mounk, Y. 2017b. Tyranny by blunder. *Slate* [online]. Available at: www.slate.com/articles/news_and_politics/the_good_fight/2017/07/donald_trump_jr_exemplifies_the_authoritarian_incompetence_of_his_father.html [Accessed August 20, 2018].

Nakamura, D. 2017. Trump's penchant for extremes worked on the campaign trail but hinders his White House. *The Washington Post* [online]. Available at: www.washingtonpost.com/politics/trumps-penchant-for-extremes-worked-on-the-campaign-trail-but-hinder-his-white-house/2017/07/19/42b3cdfa-6c78–11e7–96ab-5f38140b38cc_story.html?utm_term=.ec7b0af4de9d [Accessed August 20, 2018].

Nakayama, T.K. and Krizek. R.L. 1995. Whiteness: A strategic rhetoric. *Quarterly Journal of Speech*, 81(3), pp. 291–309.

NBC News. 2017. President Donald Trump's inaugural address (full speech) [video online]. Available at: www.youtube.com/watch?v=ThtRvBUBpQ4 [Accessed July 10 2018].

Nussbaum, M.C. 2010. *From disgust to humanity: Sexual orientation and constitutional law*. New York: Oxford University Press.

Oprea, M.G. 2016. How rich guy Donald Trump speaks working-class language. *The Federalist* [online]. Available at: thefederalist.com/2016/03/10/how-rich-guy-donald-trump-speaks-working-class-language/ [Accessed August 20, 2018].

Ott, B.L. 2017. Affect. In: J.F. Nussbaum, ed. *Oxford research encyclopedia of communication*. New York: Oxford University Press.

Parker, A. 2018. Trump seems to be saying more and more things that aren't true. *The Washington Post* [online]. Available at: www.washingtonpost.com/politics/president-trump-seems-to-be-saying-more-and-more-things-that-arent-true/2018/06/19/c1bb8af6-73d5-11e8-805c-4b67019fcfe4_story.html?utm_term=.7c1210dd171b [Accessed August 20, 2018].

PBS News Hour. 2015. Watch Donald Trump announce his candidacy for U.S. Presidency [video online]. Available at: www.youtube.com/watch?v=SpMJx0-HyOM [Accessed July 10, 2018].

Pettigrew, T.F. 2017. Social psychological perspectives on Trump Supporters. *Journal of Social and Political Psychology*, 5(1), pp. 107–116.

Philipsen, G. 1986. Mayor Daley's city council speech: A cultural analysis. *Quarterly Journal of Speech*, 72, pp. 247–260.

Porter, T. 2018. Trump aide Stephen Miller describes immigrant child separation policy as 'simple decision.' *Newsweek* [online]. Available at: www.newsweek.com/trump-aide-stephen-miller-driving-force-behind-border-child-separation-policy-980409 [Accessed August 20, 2018].

President Bannon? 2017. *New York Times* [online]. Available at: www.nytimes.com/2017/01/30/opinion/president-bannon.html [Accessed August 20, 2018].

Prose, F. 2017. Nothing about the Trump presidency is normal. Keep remembering that. *Guardian* [online]. Available at: www.theguardian.com/commentisfree/2017/jul/20/nothing-normal-trump-presidency-remember-that [Accessed August 20, 2018].

Roberts-Miller, P. 2005. Democracy, demagoguery, and critical rhetoric. *Rhetoric and Public Affairs*, 8(3), pp. 459–476.

Roberts-Miller, P. 2017. *Demagoguery and democracy*. New York: The Experiment.

Romm, J. 2016. Donald Trump may sound like a clown, but he is a rhetoric pro like Cicero. *ThinkProgress* [online]. Available at: thinkprogress.org/donald-trump-may-sound-like-a-clown-but-he-is-a-rhetoric-pro-like-cicero-ac40fd1cda79 [Accessed August 20, 2018].

Rubin, T. 2016. *Trump has no regard for rule of law. Philly.com* [online]. Available at: www.philly.com/philly/columnists/trudy_rubin/20161013_Worldview_

Rubin__Trump_has_no_regard_for_rule_of_law.html [Accessed August 20, 2018].

Salama, V. and Pace, J. 2017. Trump has embraced autocratic leaders without hesitation. *AP News* [online]. Available at: apnews.com/e7c0c828a220 431a9575e43648d032f2/trump-has-embraced-autocratic-leaders-without-hesitation [Accessed August 20, 2018].

Scalia, C.J. 2016. Donald Trump is a pragmatist, too. *The Washington Post* 29, May, p. B01.

Schmidt, S. 2017. Breaking down Trump's 'shove.' *The Washington Post* [online]. Available at: www.washingtonpost.com/news/morning-mix/wp/2017/05/26/breaking-down-trumps-shove-the-internet-debates-and-montenegros-leader-shrugs/?utm_term=.6710708221b5 [Accessed July 9, 2018].

Schmitt, M. 2016. What Trump exposed about the G.O.P. *New York Times* [online]. Available at: www.nytimes.com/2016/11/11/opinion/identity-over-ideology.html?mcubz=2 [Accessed August 20, 2018].

Schneider, C. 2017. The conservative guide to impeaching Trump. *USA Today* [online]. Available at: www.usatoday.com/story/opinion/2017/03/17/conservative-guide-impeaching-trump-christian-schneider-column/99256148/ [Accessed August 20, 2018].

Schulberg, J., Blumenthal, P., and Stein, S. 2017. Can Trump fake his way through foreign crises? We'll find out. *HuffPost.* [online]. Available at: www.huffingtonpost.com/entry/donald-trump-foreign-policy-ignorance_us_58e5589ce4b06a4cb30ee5f3 [Accessed August 20, 2018].

Shantz, J. 2017. On the messy psychology of Trumpism: Deception, the right, and neoliberal trauma. *ICD* [online]. Available at: itsgoingdown.org/messy-psychology-trumpism-deception-right-neoliberal-trauma/ [Accessed August 20, 2018].

Singer, M. 2015. Donald Trump wasn't a textbook demagogue. Until now. *The Washington Post* [online]. Available at: www.washingtonpost.com/posteverything/wp/2015/12/02/donald-trump-wasnt-a-textbook-demagogue-until-now/?utm_term=.a50ab1e6238f [Accessed August 20, 2018].

Spinoza, B. 1992. *Ethics: Treatise on the emendation of the intellect and selected letters*, trans. S. Shirley. Indianapolis: Hackett Publishing Company.

Sullivan, M. 2017. Forget Putin. Fox News and Trump is the biggest romance in politics. *The Washington Post* [online]. Available at:www.washingtonpost.com/lifestyle/style/forget-putin-fox-news-and-trump-is-the-biggest-romance-in-politics/2017/01/18/b891d7e6-dd90-11e6-ad42-f3375 f271c9c_story.html?utm_term=.e74762facaac [Accessed August 20, 2018].

Thrush G. and Haberman, M, 2017. Trump the dealmaker projects bravado, but behind the scenes, faces rare self-doubt. *New York Times* [online]. Available at: www.nytimes.com/2017/03/23/us/politics/trump-health-care-bill-regrets.html?_r=0 [Accessed August 20, 2018].

Today Show, 2016. Donald Trump town hall: Abortion exceptions, immigration, raising taxes (full). *Today* [video online]. Available at: www.youtube.com/watch?v=dO6MLHLIfdc [Accessed July 22, 2018].

Trip, G., Blinder, A., and Healy, J. 2017. Trump voters on Comey's ouster: Some cheers, and some fears of a cover-up. *New York Times* [online]. Available at: www.nytimes.com/2017/05/10/us/trump-voters-iowa-georgia-comey.html [Accessed August 20, 2018].

Trump, 'I have the best words.' 2017. *The Washington Post* [online]. Available at: www.washingtonpost.com/video/national/trump-i-have-the-best-words/2017/04/05/53a9ae4a-19fd-11e7-8598-9a99da559f9e_video.html?utm_term=.a8ca662b8422 [Accessed July 22 2018].

Trump TV Network. 2016. Simply amazing: Donald Trump massive rally in Wilkes-Barre, Pennsylvania (10/10/2016) full speech HD [video online]. Available at: www.youtube.com/watch?v=Tsp8tsucJvU [Accessed August 20, 2018].

Trump TV Network. 2017. President Donald Trump massive rally in Huntsville, Alabama 9/22/17 trump live speech [video online]. Available at: www.youtube.com/watch?v=WAXH_9bpLfI [Accessed 20 July 2018].

Whitson, S. and Poulakos, J. 1993. Nietzsche and the aesthetics of rhetoric. *Quarterly Journal of Speech*, 79(2), pp. 131–145.

Washington Post. 2017. Crowd chants 'lock her up' and Trump tells them to 'speak to Jeff Sessions' [video online]. Available at:www.youtube.com/watch?v=glHKAY5T6Fg [Accessed 20 July 2018].

Wells, J. 2017. Hideous or handsome? Dissecting Donald Trump's hairstyle. *Gentleman's Journal* [online]. Available at: www.thegentlemansjournal.com/article/hideous-handsome-dissecting-donald-trumps-hairstyle/ [Accessed August 20, 2018].

Williams, E.A. 2015. Bakhtin and *Borat*: The rogue, the clown, and the fool in carnival film. *Philament*, 20, pp. 105–128.

Wolson, P. 2017. Trump's narcissism: A key to his success and tragic flaw. *HuffPost* [online]. Available at: www.huffingtonpost.com/entry/trumps-narcissism-a-key-to-his-success-and-tragic_us_59581d34e4b0f078efd98a93 [Accessed July 11, 2017]

Woodward, G.C. 2017. The President's rhetorical style. *The Perfect Response* [online]. Available at: theperfectresponse.pages.tcnj.edu/2017/02/19/trumps-rhetoric/ [Accessed August 20, 2018].

World Wide Videos. 2016. Hilarious Donald Trump to Obama: You're fired—Raleigh, N.C. Campaign rally speech [video online]. Available at: www.youtube.com/watch?v=9_5jbZRz0mY [Accessed August 20, 2018].

Zauzmer, J. and McMillan, K. 2018. Sessions cites Bible passage used to defend slavery in defense of separating immigrant families. *The Washington Post* [online]. Available at:www.washingtonpost.com/news/acts-of-faith/wp/2018/06/14/jeff-sessions-points-to-the-bible-in-defense-of-separating-immigrant-families/?utm_term=.f753c777afb5 [Accessed August 20, 2018].

3   Trump Tweets

On November 10, 2012, Donald Trump tweeted, "Thanks-many are saying I'm the best 140 character writer in the world." As a number of Twitter users were quick to point out, it was not clear that anyone had ever said that. Jim Spellman (2012), for instance, tweeted, "FYI 'Many' is twitter slang for 'No one' @realDonaldTrump," while Leslie Abravanel (2012) responded, "when he says 'many', he means the voices in his overinflated, inexplicably coiffed head, right?" But Jon Sosis (2012) was the most incredulous, tweeting, "@realDonaldTrump You're not even the best 140 character writer in your car right now. Shut your trap you waste of life." As doubtful as it is that anyone other than Donald Trump ever declared Donald Trump "the best 140-character writer in the world," we are quite comfortable granting him this "honor," for as Virginia Heffernan (2016) notes, "Trump . . . makes himself heard in fragments, monosyllables and exclamation points, a proud male hysteric with the deafening staccato and hair-trigger immune system that Twitter exists to host." Personally, we are willing to go even further and say that Trump's manner of speaking and Twitter's underlying logic, as a modality or medium of communication, are virtually homologous.

As anecdotal evidence of this structural similarity, consider that in March 2016, MIT scientist Brad Hayes programmed a Twitterbot to mimic then candidate Trump. The bot, which is called DeepDrumpf, "uses an artificial intelligence algorithm based on Trump's language in hundreds of hours of debate transcripts" to generate Trump-like tweets (Garfield 2016). According to Hayes, Trump's debate rhetoric during the Republican primary displayed three prominent traits: it "use[d] simple language," it "defer[red] to trusted friends and colleagues," and it "constantly insult[ed] his opponents" (quoted in Garfield 2016). Though DeepDrumpf was not "taught any rules about the English language," it nonetheless managed to generate these "terrifyingly real" tweets (Biggs 2016):

- "I'd like to beat that @HillaryClinton. She is a horror. I told my supporter Putin to say that all the time. He has been amazing" (April 5, 2016).

- "If I get elected president, believe me folks. I will bring unbelievable aggression. I bring that out in people. @tedcruz #Trump2016" (April 27, 2016).

- "I can destroy a man's life by firing him over the wall. That's always been what I'm running, to kill people and create jobs. @HillaryClinton" (May 5, 2016).

Importantly, DeepDrumpf learned to create Trump-like tweets not by emulating Trump's Twitter feed, but by studying 42 pages of debate transcripts, which suggests that Trump's general style of speaking reflects the underlying logic of Twitter.

Identifying that logic is among our central aims in this chapter. Drawing upon medium theory, we identify and explain Twitter's three defining characteristics as a communication technology: simplicity, impulsivity, and incivility. From there, we turn our attention to Donald Trump's use of Twitter, comparing and contrasting his tweets as a citizen, presidential candidate, and ultimately as the commander in chief. In each of these three contexts, we categorize Trump's tweets according to the central rhetorical function they perform. The method for identifying these categories was grounded analysis, meaning that we reviewed hundreds of tweets in each of the three contexts (citizen, candidate, and president), observing and cataloging significant patterns, until no new patterns emerged. We then went back to the president's Twitter feed looking for exemplars in each of these categories. Based on analysis of those exemplars, we demonstrate that while the underlying temperament and tone of his tweeting has remained relatively stable over time, the function of his tweets shifted in subtle but significant ways depending upon the context. We begin, though, by examining Twitter as a distinctive medium of communication.

Understanding the Logic of Twitter: A Medium Theory Perspective

Media ecology or "medium theory" is a perspective that suggests every communication technology (i.e., medium) has key physical, psychological, and social features that are relatively distinct and fixed, and that these features shape how users of that medium communicate, process information, and make sense of the world (Meyrowitz 1994). In short, every communication medium trains us to think and, thus, to speak in particular ways. We maintain that Twitter ultimately trains us to devalue others, thereby cultivating mean and malicious discourse. To understand how it does this, we examine Twitter's defining features. Much like Facebook's "status updates," Twitter is a microblogging platform, "a form of blogging in which entries typically consist of short content such as phrases, quick comments, images, or links to videos" (Stieglitz and Dang-Xuan 2013, p. 219). In the case of Twitter, users send and receive "tweets," messages consisting of no more than 140 characters (the number was doubled to 280 on November 7, 2017). Since its launch in March 2006, Twitter has grown rapidly in popularity, and by 2014 it had more than 500 million users who were generating over 400 million tweets a day (Zubiaga et al. 2015, p. 462). As a mode of communication, Twitter is defined by three key features: simplicity, impulsivity, and incivility.

Twitter Demands Simplicity

Despite the recent doubling of its character limitation (from 140 to 280), Twitter's highly restricted form structurally disallows the communication of detailed and sophisticated messages. To be clear, a tweet may be clever or witty, but it cannot be complex. On election night, for instance, Jason Sweeny (2016) tweeted, "I can't imagine how stressed Americans are feeling right now. I'm Canadian and I'm chugging maple syrup and just punched a moose." While this tweet humorously captures the anxiety (and anger and sheer terror) that many felt on election night, it does not and cannot explain, analyze, or assess those feelings. In his book *Amusing Ourselves to Death*, medium theorist Neil Postman (1985) points to smoke signals as an example of a communication technology whose form structurally prevents the communication of complex content such as philosophical argument. "Puffs of smoke," he writes,

> are insufficiently complex to express ideas on the nature of existence, and even if they were not, a Cherokee philosopher would run short of either wood or blankets long before he reached his second axiom. You cannot use smoke to do philosophy.
>
> (p. 7)

With respect to its capacity to convey complex ideas and concepts, Twitter is the modern-day equivalent of smoke signals, which explains why one can philosophize *about* Twitter but not philosophize *on* Twitter.

Perhaps the best evidence that Twitter is ill equipped to handle complex content is the common practice of linking. Twitter users often post links to videos, news articles, government reports, and research studies because the ideas contained in those messages are far too complex to be conveyed without the link. When clever and even smart ideas are expressed on Twitter, the form demands that they are greatly simplified; and the repeated production and consumption of simple messages, which endlessly redirect our attention elsewhere via hyperlinks, reshapes human cognition in ways that nurture simple-mindedness and promote short attention spans. Indeed, the culture of the internet in general tends to promote "'shallow' information processing behaviors characterized by rapid attention shifting and reduced deliberations" (Loh and Kanai 2015). Just as the invention and spread of writing gave rise to the literate mind, destroying memory, the development and growth of social media has the ushered in the distracted mind (Carr 2010). By demanding simplicity, Twitter undermines our ability to talk about and, thus, to think about issues and events in more complex ways (Kapko 2016).

Twitter Promotes Impulsivity

While Twitter is similar to smoke signals in terms of message complexity, it is utterly dissimilar in terms of effort. When one decides to send a smoke signal, one must go to considerable effort (i.e., gathering wood, building a fire, and going to a location where the smoke can be seen at a great distance). If one chooses to go to all that effort, one presumably has something important to communicate and, in fact, smoke signals have historically been used as a means of signaling impending danger. Tweeting, by contrast, requires almost no effort at all. It is ridiculously easy. Thanks to wireless technology, one can tweet from virtually anywhere at any time. Since tweeting requires little effort, it requires little forethought, reflection, or consideration of consequences. Tweeting is, in short, a highly impulsive activity, something that one can do easily even if one has nothing considered or important to say. Tweets are often sparked by an affective charge, a charge that they transfer through the social network since "emotionally charged Twitter messages tend to be retweeted more often and more quickly compared to neutral ones" (Stieglitz and Dang-Xuan 2013, p. 217).

Repeated use of Twitter trains users to speak impetuously, which may partially account for why visiting NYU professor Geoffrey Miller tweeted: "Dear obese PhD applicants: if you didn't have the willpower to stop eating carbs, you won't have the willpower to do a dissertation #truth" (June 2, 2013), or why public relations executive Justine Stacco tweeted: "Going to Africa. Hope I don't get AIDS. Just Kidding. I'm white!" (December 13, 2013), or why Minnesota State Representative Pat Garofalo tweeted: "Let's be honest, 70% of teams in NBA could fold tomorrow + nobody would notice a difference w/ possible exception of increase in streetcrime" (March 9, 2014). A professor, a PR executive, and an elected official should know better than to engage in fat-shaming and racism, and judging from their public apologies, they probably do. That they tweeted these comments despite knowing better suggests just how much Twitter's form inhibits reflexivity.

Twitter Fosters Incivility

Uncivil communication refers to speech that is impolite, insulting, or otherwise offensive. Two dimensions of Twitter, in particular, encourage uncivil discourse. First, Twitter is decidedly informal. Its lack of concern with proper grammar and style undermines norms that tend to enforce civility. The act of writing "Dear So-and-So" at the start of a formal letter, for instance, lessens the likelihood that demeaning communication will follow. Second, Twitter "depersonalizes interactions," creating a context in which "people do not consider how their interactions will affect others" (Tait 2016). It is much easier to say something nasty about someone when they are not physically present. Take, for example, rapper Azealia Banks' racist and homophobic tweets about former One Direction singer Zayn Malik. Had Malik been present, it is hard to imagine that Banks would have said, "dude, I make better music than you. Simmer down with that fake white boy rebellion and that wannabe Bieber swag. Lol u a bitch nigga for even responding like that" or "Imma start calling you punjab you dirty bitch. You a dick rider for real. Ride this dick until the wheels fall off Punjab." Twitter's lack of formality and intimacy undermines the social norms that uphold civility and predisposes users to engage in both divisive and derisive communication.

We recognize, of course, that not all content on Twitter is equally harmful. Much of the Twittersphere is relatively innocuous; its content is so trite, vacuous, and insignificant as to be of little consequence, or at least of little consequence beyond providing an outlet for narcissists to post "messages relating to themselves or their thoughts" (Stieglitz and

Dang-Xuan 2013, p. 220). One study suggests that about 80 percent of the activity on Twitter falls in this category (Naaman et al. 2010). The danger arises from the other 20 percent when issues of social, cultural, and political import are filtered through the lens of Twitter, for Twitter infects public discourse like a social cancer. It destroys dialog and deliberation, fosters farce and fanaticism, and contributes to callousness and contempt.

Nor are Twitter's defining traits equally appealing to everyone. Indeed, recent research indicates a link "between Dark Triad constructs and Twitter usage" (Sumner et al. 2012, p. 386). In other words, the personality traits of narcissism, Machiavellianism, and psychopathy—also known as the Dark Triad—are positively related to Twitter usage. Since the messages on Twitter are neither complex nor considered, heavy Twitter users are not generally motivated by the fact that they have something significant to say. They rarely do. What tends to motivate them is self-interest and self-promotion. Above all, frequent Twitter users appear to have a desperate, even compulsive, need for attention, and to ensure that they get that attention, "they tend to post more emotionally charged tweets" (Stieglitz and Dang-Xuan 2013, p. 241). While emotion ranges from positive to negative, heavy Twitter users favor negativity, which reinforces a study that found "negative sentiment" is the key to popularity on Twitter (Thelwall et al. 2011, p. 415). All of this means that Twitter breeds dark, degrading, and dehumanizing discourse; it breeds vitriol and violence; in short, it breeds Donald Trump.

Assessing @realDonaldTrump

In the introduction to this chapter, we suggested that there is a rather strong homology between the president's general manner of speaking and the logic of Twitter as a technology of communication. Analysts who have studied Trump's public discourse have observed speech patterns that correspond closely with what we have identified as Twitter's three defining features: simplicity, impulsivity, and incivility. With respect to simplicity, Jack Shafer (2015) writes, "Trump isn't a simpleton, he just talks like one. . . . [he] resists multisyllabic words and complex, writerly sentence constructions when speaking extemporaneously in a debate, at a news conference or in an interview."

When Trump's public discourse is measured against the Flesch—Kincaid grade-level test, it rates at a third-or fourth-grade reading level. Trump's speech is also decidedly impulsive. Reflecting on how Trump's speech favors the momentary over the considered, Neal Gabler (2016) wrote during the campaign, "Above all else, Donald Trump is the candidate of impulse running against candidates of calculation." Finally, much of Trump's discourse lacks basic civility. Based on an analysis of Trump's public utterances during the campaign, Jeremy Merrill (2015) concluded, "Mr. Trump's language is darker, more violent and more prone to insults." The homology between Trump's public rhetoric and the logic of Twitter suggests that Trump's popularity is due, at least in part, to the fact that "He is a man of his technological moment" (Gabler 2016). It may also account for the popularity of Trump's Twitter account, @realDonaldTrump, which had more than 54 million followers as of this writing, though as many as 79 percent of those are believed to be fake or inactive (Bilton 2016; Petersen 2016).

Since, as we have argued, simplicity, impulsivity, and incivility are defining traits of Twitter as a modality of communication, one will find evidence of these traits in the habits of frequent Twitter users. What makes Trump somewhat distinctive from other heavy Twitter users is twofold. First, in the case of Trump, one also finds these traits in modes of communication, such as public speeches, where you would not expect to find them. Such traits are, to the contrary, generally atypical of presidential communication (from inaugural addresses to State of the Union speeches). Second, these traits are evident in Trump's Twitter habits over time, even though his primary purposes and motivations for using Twitter have shifted somewhat. The bulk of our analysis in this chapter seeks to identify those shifts, mapping them across three key contexts: citizen Trump, candidate Trump, and President Trump. Table 3.1 summarizes the central rhetorical aims of Trump's Twitter behavior in each of those contexts.

Citizen Trump: The Self-Promotional Use of Twitter

Prior to his election as president, Donald Trump was best known for playing a tough business negotiator and successful real-estate developer on two NBC reality TV series: *The Apprentice* and *The Celebrity Apprentice*. Long before becoming a prominent reality television personality though, Trump had learned that "success" in the information age is as much about projecting an image of success as it is about accomplishing anything substantive and measurable (such as the generation of wealth or a demonstrated ability to negotiate good business deals). As such, throughout his life and career, Trump has consistently exaggerated his wealth and business acumen to project the image of a highly successful businessperson. So, prior to his official entry into politics, Trump used Twitter principally for

Table 3.1 Trump's evolving Twitter behavior

Context	Central Rhetorical Aims		
Citizen Trump (January 1, 2013 to December 31, 2014)	1. Branding— promotional statements aimed at marketing Trump products and properties	2. Boasting— self-ingratiating statements aimed at fostering an image of success/winning	3. Bullying— abusive statements aimed at appearing "tough" through intimidation
Candidate Trump (June 16, 2015 to November 8, 2016)	1. Defining— sloganeering aimed at promoting a unified and unifying political vision	2. Disrupting— subversive statements aimed at demonstrating anti-establishment credentials	3. Demeaning— derogatory statements aimed at uncrowning political elites
President Trump (January 20, 2017 to September 1, 2018)	1. Dissembling— deceitful statements aimed at manipulating public opinion	2. Distracting— shocking statements aimed at redirecting public attention	3. Discrediting— disparaging statements aimed at undermining others' credibility

the purpose of cultivating that image. "Like many public figures," Nicholas Carr (2018) explains, Trump, who sent his first tweet in 2009, "set up his account for marketing purposes . . . . to promote his TV show, . . . and his latest book, . . . along with his various businesses and other interests." Based on our analysis of Trump's Twitter feed from January 1, 2013 to December 31, 2014, we found that Trump employed three main rhetorical devices to promote an image of success: branding, boasting, and bullying. While we will discuss each of these devices separately, it is worth noting that they are deeply intertwined and, in fact, many of his tweets during this period demonstrate more than one of these devices.

Branding

This category of tweets serves a marketing purpose, which is to foster, promote, and reinforce the "Trump brand." As much as Trump campaigned against elitism in 2016, the defining feature of his brand has long been distinction, and, as such, Trump endlessly markets his products and properties as being of the highest quality, involving the best materials, locations, etc., and reflecting refined tastes and sensibilities. This is evident in Trump's own tweets, which clearly and consistently associate the Trump brand with an image of distinction. Table 3.2 identifies ten tweets that fall into the category of branding; they feature various terms of distinction such as "masterpiece," "finest," "award winning," "superior quality," "perfection," "incredible," "beautiful," "highest rated," "premiere," "sophistication," "elegant," "world-class," "excellence," "iconic," "luxurious," "elite," "pinnacle," and "prestige." But the most frequently used term of distinction, which appears in 46 separate tweets during the two-year period that we dubbed "citizen Trump," is "signature." This term, which is part of the official name of many Trump-branded products, suggests that Trump products and properties are, at once, exceptional and exclusive. It is a message Trump reinforced through repetition, and in 2013–14, for instance, he tweeted about the Trump National Doral Miami a total of 220 times, which is more than once every three days.

Boasting

Whereas Trump's tweets directed at branding appeal to elitist sensibilities through classist constructions of distinction, his tweets characterized by boasting serve as self-congratulatory statements aimed at reinforcing his image as a successful dealmaker and real-estate developer. As the tweets in Table 3.3 demonstrate, Trump repeatedly reminds his Twitter followers that he is making "big deals" and doing "major business deals" as a way fostering an image of business success, which he reinforces with frequent reference to specific multimillion-dollar figures and hyperbolic claims about the greatness of his properties (i.e., "a masterpiece," "perhaps the greatest ever built!" and "one of the great hotels anywhere in the world"). While his fixation on the size of his deals and the greatness of his properties, no doubt, masks deeply held insecurities, it also affirms Trump's self-styled image of himself as important and successful, as do his repeated narcissistic references to his television appearances (i.e., "Fox & Friends" and Gretchen Carlson's "new Fox show"). Though we have not included any examples in Table 3.3, Trump also tweeted 646 times—nearly once per day—about *The Apprentice/Celebrity Apprentice* during this two-year window.

Table 3.2 Branding—citizen Trump (Jan. 1, 2013–Dec. 31, 2014)

Tweet	Date/Time	Likes	Retweets
Open for the 2014 season Mar-a-Lago Club is an architectural masterpiece offering the finest amenities in the world http://t.co/Oa3jE1MGPq	Nov. 19, 2014 11:54 AM	46	31
@TrumpDoral offers multiple award winning dining options in our all-new signature restaurant and lounges http://t.co/7Tgnnje2eR	July 22, 2014 11:29 AM	20	28
Trump Tower Punta Del Este features the Trump Organization's signature superior quality, detail & perfection http://t.co/wRVyIzdLsz	June 25, 2014 1:04 PM	26	36
I pick the best locations-@Trump_ Charlotte has incredible views of beautiful Lake Norman. http://t.co/Lnlfq3wyXf	April 16, 2014 10:13 AM	58	34
@WineEnthusiast's highest rated wine in Virginia, @trumpwinery is the premier name in sophistication and quality http://t.co/Tas3Dhp9hH	Feb. 04, 2014 10:46 AM	4	6
Rated Toronto's #1 hotel, @TrumpTO has 261 guest rooms & suites furnished in elegant, cosmopolitan style. http://t.co/fogCH2mx2c	Dec. 20, 2013 10:21 AM	20	35
W/ signature Trump amenities, 5 star rooms & world-class restaurants, @TrumpWaikiki brings excellence to Hawaii http://t.co/sawW8bGjBZ	Nov. 18, 2013 9:50 AM	24	22
An iconic building and top tourist attraction, @TrumpTowerNY sets New York City's luxury standard http://t.co/JrjBe4aRat & great food!	Oct. 7, 2013 9:13 AM	18	13
Five Star @TrumpCondosLV are the most luxurious & elite residences in the Vegas market http://t.co/xQZ3Lu-ZHd4 "If you love it, own it"	Sept. 27, 2013 8:31 AM	13	13
The Trump Signature Collection, exclusively available at @Macys, is the pinnacle of style and prestige http://t.co/mahENjAx8f	Aug. 9, 2013 3:27 PM	23	19

Table 3.3 Boasting—citizen Trump (Jan. 1, 2013–Dec. 31, 2014)

Tweet	Date/Time	Likes	Retweets
Deals are my art form. Other people paint beautifully or write poetry. I like making deals preferably big deals. That's how I get my kicks.	Dec. 29, 2014 7:39 AM	14,572	7,670
So sad that Burt Reynolds has lost all of his money. I wish he came to me for advice—he would be rich as hell!	Dec. 02, 2014 7:55 AM	468	272
Sorry, won't be doing Fox & Friends this morning—will be in India on a couple of major business deals!	Aug. 11, 2014 3:16 AM	115	74
People often ask me the secret to my success, and the answer is simple: passion, focus and hard work. Momentum keeps it all going.	Jan. 20, 2014 12:08 PM	651	790
Just left $259 million rebuilding of Doral in Miami. Amazing—Trump National Doral will be a master-piece (if I do say so myself)!	Nov. 30, 2013 1:33 PM	126	73
Congrats @GretchenCarlson's new Fox show debuts w/ very strong ratings http://t.co/IhmmXHig9r Guess who her first guest was? Donald Trump.	Oct. 2, 2013 11:15 AM	32	34
More and more reporters are using the word TRUMP when referring to winning—just used on Bloomberg News. Gee, I wonder why?	July 24, 2013 6:58 AM	55	69
The people of Scotland love the golf course I have built-it is now consid-ered perhaps the greatest ever built! Thank you also to Robb Report	June 26, 2013 4:41 AM	37	42
I've done the largest house sale in U.S. history by selling a Palm Beach mansion for $100M, $60M more than I paid. I love real estate.	June 5, 2013 1:28 PM	366	625
The Old Post Office building in Washington (D.C.) will soon be transformed into one of the great hotels anywhere in the world-lots of jobs!	Aug. 5, 2013 4:41 PM	68	78

Bullying

Given Twitter's tendency for incivility and Trump's propensity for bullying, that Trump would regularly use the platform to make blustery statements aimed at abusing and intimidating others is predictable. Equally predictable, given his notoriously thin skin, Trump usually directs his bullying behavior at persons or institutions who have criticized him in some manner. The precise nature of his online abuse is revealing, however. As the tweets in Table 3.4 illuminate, Trump's attacks on others nearly always point to flaws in his own character. Trump's frequent criticism of women's intelligence and looks (i.e., "dummy" or "dumb" and "ugly" and "frumpy"), for instance, highlights his misogynistic beliefs, as well as his insecurities about his own intelligence and appearance. Similarly, a pair of tweets claiming that *Touré* Neblett and Bryant Gumbel are "racists" highlights his own racism. Putting aside the fact that both men are African American, the tweets conclude by criticizing the men for what Trump clearly regards as a far more damning offense: lack of televisual success (i.e., "bad ratings" and "Failed at CBS"). In lumping together and, thereby, suggesting some moral equivalency between being a racist and having low television ratings, Trump reveals his own racist attitudes. Once the mirror-like logic of Trump's Twitter-bullying is unlocked, it quickly becomes obvious that his other insults (i.e., "mentally sick," "loser," "delusional," "asshole," "incompetent," "lightweight" and "pathetic") are little more than unconscious self-indictments. Nevertheless, the insults function rhetorically to perpetuate Trump's image as a hard-hitting, tough-guy.

Candidate Trump: The Tactical Use of Twitter

In the previous section, we showed how Donald Trump used Twitter during 2013–14 to manufacture the persona of a tough-guy businessperson and shrewd dealmaker whose products and properties reflect "sophisticated" (read: aging and white) tastes. Citizen Trump was ten times more likely to tweet about golf (409 times) than illegal immigrants/immigration (41 tweets) in that two-year period. It would be a mistake, however, to suggest that Trump was not concerned with politics at all during that time. In addition to regularly tweeting about political figures and issues such as Karl Rove (19 times), Democrats (27 times), taxes (35 times), Vladimir Putin (40 times), Republicans (76 times), Iraq (81 times), and global warming (83 times), Trump tweeted obsessively—more than once a day—about President Obama (969 times). Notably, there was not a single tweet about fake news.

Table 3.4 Bullying—citizen Trump (Jan. 1, 2013–Dec. 31, 2014)

Tweet	Date/Time	Likes	Retweets
Sorry, @Rosie is a mentally sick woman, a bully, a dummy and, above all, a loser. Other than that she is just wonderful!	Dec. 8, 2014 5:53 PM	1,876	1,213
Dennis Rodman was either drunk or on drugs (delusional) when he said I wanted to go to North Korea with him. Glad I fired him on Apprentice!	May 07, 2014 6:39 PM	3,716	2,497
Huffington Post is just upset that I said its purchase by AOL has been a disaster and that Arianna Huffington is ugly both inside and out!	April 20, 2014 4:57 PM	380	388
Major League Baseball was really smart when they wouldn't let Mark Cuban buy a team. Was it his financials or the fact that he's an asshole?	April 05, 2014 11:40 AM	2,425	1,700
Frumpy and very dumb Gail Collins an editorial writer at The New York Times is so lucky to even have a job. Check her out—incompetent!	March 15, 2014 2:31 PM	82	60
Lightweight @AGSchneiderman's phony lawsuit against Trump U was decimated by the court—he's a loser!	Feb. 27, 2014 6:43 AM	114	129
If Graydon Carter's very dumb bosses would fire him for his terrible circulation numbers at failing Vanity Fair-his bad food restaurants die	Dec. 10, 2013 5:59 AM	28	18
@Toure Dumb as a rock Toure doesn't have a clue about money or anything else-merely a simpleton racist. Really bad ratings, really stupid guy	Sept. 9, 2013 6:53 PM	47	42
You must admit that Bryant Gumbel is one of the dumbest racists around—an arrogant dope with no talent. Failed at CBS etc-why still on TV?	Aug. 21, 2013 8:21 PM	114	154
She is so sad and pathetic that I almost feel sorry for Sec.Sebelius. She has done great harm to many people and must be fired. Incompetent!	July 11, 2013 6:23 PM	150	165

In the six months leading up to Trump's racist statement announcing his run for president, Trump's Twitterfeed became increasing political. But because this marks a period of transition, our analysis of the Twitter period we call "candidate Trump" is limited to the time between his formal announcement (June 16, 2015) and his election-night victory (November 8, 2016). During that period, Trump's use of Twitter shifted from self-promotion of the Trump brand to the tactical positioning of himself as the anti-establishment candidate. We use the term "tactical" to highlight that Trump was, in fact, a political outsider who operated largely independent of—or perhaps more accurately, in the cracks and crevices of—the political system and its normative constraints. In retrospect, the tactical freedom to transgress political norms turned out to be a significant advantage for Trump, who repurposed his Twitterfeed to reflect three new rhetorical ends: defining, disrupting, and demeaning.

Defining

One of the central elements of political campaigns is the campaign slogan, a motto or saying that serves to "define" and promote a unified and unifying political vision. It functions much like a product brand, but is typically more generic, tapping into a broad cultural style or zeitgeist. Inevitably, campaign slogans express an affective frame, of which there are two basic orientations: for and against (Burke 1984, pp. 3–4). Trump's campaign slogan—"Make America Great Again" (MAGA)—is a frame of rejection, an explicit protest *against* the status quo, and thus falls on the negative side of this binary. It is also poached, a shameless derivative of the 1980 Reagan/Bush campaign phrase "Let's Make America Great Again." When asked about the similarity between the two slogans in 2017, Trump pretended not to know, spinning a transparent lie about having "invented" it after Mitt Romney lost to Barack Obama in 2012. As he was pressed on the issue, Trump said of Reagan, "But he didn't trademark it" (Tumulty 2017), which tellingly suggests that he was aware of the original.

The tweets that fall into the category we call "defining" all work to operationalize the slogan "Make America Great Again." But they do something even more fundamental as well. By invoking the politics of white rage, they appeal to angry white voters on a primarily visceral level, mobilizing their frustration and disenchantment with the status quo. The phrase MAGA implies that America was formerly great, but that it has lost its greatness (or more precisely, for Trump, that a black president has tarnished it). Consequently, as the sample tweets in Table 3.5 demonstrate, Trump regularly painted a dark (and

Table 3.5 Defining—candidate Trump (June 16, 2015–Nov. 8, 2016)

Tweet	Date/Time	Likes	Retweets
Get out and vote! I am your voice and I will fight for you! We will make America great again! https://t.co/XXvLRlhSaz	Oct. 25, 2016 7:44 AM	25,261	12,203
What do African-Americans and Hispanics have to lose by going with me. Look at the poverty crime and educational statistics. I will fix it!	Aug. 26, 2016 7:20 AM	28,754	9,907
Vast numbers of manufacturing jobs in Pennsylvania have moved to Mexico and other countries. That will end when I win!	Aug. 1, 2016 6:33 PM	25,348	7,978
People very unhappy with Crooked Hillary and Obama on JOBS and SAFETY! Biggest trade deficit in many years! More attacks will follow Orlando	June 17, 2016 4:20 AM	20,950	6,733
The economy is bad and getting worse-almost ZERO growth this quarter. Nobody can beat me on the economy (and jobs). MAKE AMERICA GREAT AGAIN	April 30, 2016 10:21 AM	20,895	7,666
The United States cannot continue to make such bad, one-sided trade deals. There are only so many jobs we can give up. No more!	March 27, 2016 6:17 PM	20,823	6,733
Nobody will protect our Nation like Donald J. Trump. Our military will be greatly strengthened and our borders will be strong. Illegals out	March 26, 2016 12:20 PM	25,404	8,971
I will be the greatest job-producing president in American history. #Trump2016 #VoteTrump https://t.co/tykxcT5ZtG https://t.co/oc480lwVQg	Jan. 23, 2016 5:57 AM	7,371	2,723
We must stop the crime and killing machine that is illegal immigration. Rampant problems will only get worse. Take back our country!	Aug. 10, 2015 5:58 PM	6,967	3,372
We MUST have strong borders and stop illegal immigration. Without that we do not have a country. Also, Mexico is killing U.S. on trade. WIN!	June 30, 2015 5:35 AM	2,089	1,266

racist) vision of America, ranting and raving about illegal immigration and increasing crime rates, job loss and poor economic opportunities, one-sided trade deals and crippling trade deficits, and a weakened military and growing terrorist threats. It did not matter that the facts were rarely on Trump's side because his aggrieved, invective-spewing outlook on Obama's America "felt" real to Trump followers. In addition to painting a bleak picture of America, Trump cast himself as the solution (i.e., "I am your voice," "I will fix it," "Nobody will protect our Nation like Donald J. Trump," and "I will be the greatest job-producing president in American history").

Disrupting

In addition to using Twitter to define (invent) a problem, namely American decline, Trump employed the platform to play the role of the anti-establishment candidate. He consistently linked American decline with the political status quo, which lent his outsider status as a businessperson (rather than as a career politician) a special credibility. Table 3.6 shows how Trump adopted the persona of disrupter, pitting himself against "political hacks," "the swamp," "Washington insiders," "the puppets of politics," "lobbyists and special interests," and, most of all, "the Establishment." As important as Trump's message of disruption was to his success, so, too, was his mode of communicating it. The frequency with which Trump used Twitter during the campaign was itself disruptive, a subversion of political norms. Not only did social media allow him to bypass the mainstream media by messaging voters directly, but it also challenged the view of political campaigns as massive corporate-funded, public relations operations beholden to special interests and to political correctness. Simply put, his unfiltered, uninhibited use of Twitter challenged the view of politicians as "polished" and inauthentic. One study found:

> that more than one-third of [his] tweets included 'authenticity markers', in the sense that they expressed impoliteness and political incorrectness, often using capital letters. . . . Capital letters are often used to emphasise one's sincerity, spontaneity and engagement, offering the speaker an air of authenticity.
>
> (Enli 2017, p. 58)

Trump, a man who his spent his entire career promoting a carefully constructed brand image, managed to appear more authentic than traditional political candidates by regularly using a communication

Table 3.6 Disrupting—candidate Trump (June 16, 2015–Nov. 8, 2016)

Tweet	Tweet	Tweet	Tweet
USA has the greatest business people in the world but we let political hacks negotiate our deals. We need change! #BigLeagueTruth #Debate	Oct. 19, 2016 7:28 PM	19,184	7,847
I will Make Our Government Honest Again—believe me. But first, I'm going to have to #DrainTheSwamp in DC. https://t.co/m1lMAQPnIb	Oct. 18, 2016 8:33 AM	25,245	12,771
It is so nice that the shackles have been taken off me and I can now fight for America the way I want to.	Oct. 11, 2016 9:00 AM	59,422	22,399
I know our complex tax laws better than anyone who has ever run for president and am the only one who can fix them. #failing@nytimes	Oct. 2, 2016 4:22 AM	37,503	14,440
I am running against the Washington insiders, just like I did in the Republican Primaries. These are the people that have made U.S. a mess!	Aug. 9, 2016 4:59 AM	43,458	15,435
I turned down a meeting with Charles and David Koch. Much better for them to meet with the puppets of politics, they will do much better!	July 30, 2016 1:01 PM	32,234	11,290
Remember, I am the only candidate who is self-funding. While I am given little credit for this by the voters, I am not bought like others!	March 26, 2016 1:16 PM	32,466	10,091
We cannot let the failing REPUBLICAN ESTABLISHMENT, who could not stop Obama (twice), ruin the MOVEMENT with millions of $'s in false ads!	March 7, 2016 5:03 AM	17,384	6,781
I am self-funding my campaign and am therefore not controlled by the lobbyists and special interests like lightweight Rubio or Ted Cruz!	Feb. 27, 2016 7:25 AM	16,606	5,624
Let's Trump the Establishment! We are no longer silent. We will Make America Great Again! https://t.co/u25yI6aIvG	July 22, 2015 12:03 PM	1,679	818

platform that is characterized by its informality, impulsivity, and incivility.

Demeaning

Among the privileges that Trump enjoyed as a political outsider during the campaign was an acceptance of his crass willingness to openly disparage and demean his foes. Trump's regular practice of assigning his political opponents derogatory nicknames only served to further enhance his anti-establishment credentials. As evidenced by the tweets in Table 3.7, Trump bucked the norms of political civility, disparaging Hillary Clinton as "crooked," Ruth Bader Ginsburg as "dumb," Elizabeth Warren as "goofy," Bernie Sanders as "crazy," Ted Cruz as a liar and "not very presidential," Megyn Kelly as "overrated & crazy," Marco Rubio as "little" and "lightweight," Rand Paul as "weird," and Frank Luntz as a "clown." Such remarks function as more than mere insults; rhetorically, they work to reaffirm the image of Trump as a straight-talker, as someone who tells it likes he sees it, and as authentic. That he was willing to behave so indignantly toward political elites fed the perception among his followers that Trump would, in fact, "drain the swamp," a popular hashtag during his campaign that referenced getting rid of career politicians in Washington, DC.

President Trump: The Strategic Use of Twitter

After his surprise election victory and subsequent inauguration, Trump necessarily went from being a political outsider to being at the center of the political establishment. While Trump tried to resist this shift in terms of his public image (by pitting himself against an establishment Congress), he simultaneously sought to exercise his newfound authority by mobilizing the awesome power of his office. Nowhere was this more evident than in Trump's early immigration efforts, in which he used executive orders to attempt, often illegally, to remake US immigration policy by banning all immigrants from select Muslim-majority countries. Despite the somewhat mixed results of these efforts, they highlight—much like the president's pardon authority—the power inherent in the executive branch.

The transition from political outsider to principal establishment figure was also evident in Trump's Twitterfeed, which inevitably shifted from the tactical to the more strategic. Suddenly, Trump could alter policy, influence foreign affairs, and move financial markets with nothing more than one of his reckless and uninformed Twitter

Table 3.7 Demeaning—candidate Trump (June 16, 2015–Nov. 8, 2016)

Tweet	Tweet	Tweet	Tweet
After decades of lies and scandal, Crooked Hillary's corruption is closing in. #DrainTheSwamp! https://t.co/YivCacmkKq	Nov. 2, 2016 12:09 PM	45,340	24,974
Justice Ginsburg of the U.S. Supreme Court has embarrassed all by making very dumb political statements about me. Her mind is shot—resign!	July 12, 2016 9:54 PM	33,393	10,965
Mitt Romney had his chance to beat a failed president but he choked like a dog. Now he calls me racist-but I am least racist person there is	June 11, 2016 4:18 AM	31,164	10,135
Pocahontas is at it again! Goofy Elizabeth Warren, one of the least productive U.S. Senators, has a nasty mouth. Hope she is V.P. choice.	June 10, 2016 5:07 AM	27,406	8,935
I don't want to hit Crazy Bernie Sanders too hard yet because I love watching what he is doing to Crooked Hillary. His time will come!	May 11, 2016 3:26 AM	29,557	9,595
Wow, Lyin' Ted Cruz really went wacko today. Made all sorts of crazy charges. Can't function under pressure—not very presidential. Sad!	May 3, 2016 4:02 PM	23,513	7,484
Highly overrated & crazy @megynkelly is always complaining about Trump and yet she devotes her shows to me. Focus on others Megyn!	March 17, 2016 9:58 AM	19,984	5,498
Little Marco Rubio, the lightweight no show Senator from Florida is just another Washington politician. https://t.co/NsLrHrqjdx	Feb. 28, 2015 9:50 AM	12,468	5,688
Truly weird Senator Rand Paul of Kentucky reminds me of a spoiled brat without a properly functioning brain. He was terrible at DEBATE!	Aug. 10, 2015 5:41 PM	5,541	2,734
.@FrankLuntz, your so-called "focus groups" are a total joke. Don't come to my office looking for business again. You are a clown!	Aug.7, 2015 12:45 AM	4,151	2,242

tantrums. To observe that Trump's tweets as president operate "strategically" is not to suggest that they are careful or considered, but to recognize that they entail "the calculation (or manipulation) of power relationships that becomes possible as soon as a subject with will and power . . . can be isolated" (de Certeau 1984, pp. 35–36). In one stunning tweet, for instance, the president claimed, "As has been stated by numerous legal scholars, I have the absolute right to PARDON myself, but why would I do that when I have done nothing wrong?" (Trump 2018). Based upon an examination of Trump's Twitter use as president (January 20, 2017 to September 1, 2018), we identify three primary rhetorical strategies: dissembling, distracting, and discrediting.

Dissembling

"Dissembling" refers to a vast category of tweets in which the president blatantly lies, pedals personal delusions and wild conspiracy theories, grossly distorts or flat out denies established and verifiable facts, and otherwise engages in total fabrications. As Andrew Sullivan (2018) recounts in *New York* magazine, just a few of the countless falsehoods that Trump has perpetuated since taking office include:

> that the economy was in free-fall until he took office, after which it soared; that he alone has brought black and Hispanic unemployment down; that his administration has accomplished more than any other at this point in its term; that Democrats colluded with the Kremlin to try to rig the election; that Robert Mueller is a closet Democrat; that climate change is a hoax; that the American-created international trading system was designed to hurt the U.S., . . . that sabotaging the ACA will lead to lower premiums, greater choice, and better health outcomes for all.

Similarly, the sample tweets in Table 3.8 show the president lying about everything from the TV ratings for his first State of the Union (SOTU) address ("45.6 million people watched the highest number in history") to tax rates ("We are the highest taxed nation in the world"), claims that are empirically verifiable as untrue. While 45.6 million people did watch Trump's SOTU speech, this ranks sixth since Nielsen started gathering data in 1993 (62 million for George W. Bush in 2003; 53 million for Bill Clinton in 1998; 51.8 million for George W. Bush in 2002; 48 million for Barack Obama in 2010; and 45.8 million for

Table 3.8 Dissembling—President Trump (Jan. 20, 2017–Sept. 1, 2018)

Tweet	Date/Time	Favorites	Retweets
Just landed—a long trip, but everybody can now feel much safer than the day I took office. There is no longer a Nuclear Threat from North Korea. Meeting with Kim Jong Un was an interesting and very positive experience. North Korea has great potential for the future!	June 13, 2018 2:56 AM	103,387	21,501
Separating families at the Border is the fault of bad legislation passed by the Democrats. Border Security laws should be changed but the Dems can't get their act together! Started the Wall.	June 5, 2018 4:58 AM	82,417	18,949
Not that it matters but I never fired James Comey because of Russia! The Corrupt Mainstream Media loves to keep pushing that narrative, but they know it is not true!	May 31, 2018 5:11 AM	74,911	16,594
Clapper has now admitted that there was Spying in my campaign. Large dollars were paid to the Spy, far beyond normal. Starting to look like one of the biggest political scandals in U.S. history. SPYGATE—a terrible thing!	May 24, 2018 5:21 AM	110,221	31,264
Thank you for all of the nice compliments and reviews on the State of the Union speech. 45.6 million people watched the highest number in history. @FoxNews beat every other Network for the first time ever with 11.7 million people tuning in. Delivered from the heart!	Feb. 1, 2018 4:02 AM	181,427	36,107
Government Funding Bill past last night in the House of Representatives. Now Democrats are needed if it is to pass in the Senate—but they want illegal immigration and weak borders. Shutdown coming? We need more Republican victories in 2018!	Jan. 19, 2018 4:04 AM	108,656	25,136
Unemployment for Black Americans is the lowest ever recorded. Trump approval ratings with Black Americans has doubled. Thank you and it will get even (much) better! @FoxNews	Jan. 16, 2018 6:30 AM	111,562	27,074

(Continued)

Table 3.8 (Continued)

Tweet	Date/Time	Favorites	Retweets
Yesterday was another big day for jobs and the Stock Market. Chrysler coming back to U.S. (Michigan) from Mexico and many more companies paying out Tax Cut money to employees. If Dems won in November, Market would have TANKED! It was headed for disaster.	Jan. 13, 2018 9:20 AM	tweet deleted	
Will be going to North Dakota today to discuss tax reform and tax cuts. We are the highest taxed nation in the world—that will change.	Sept. 6, 2017 3:47 AM	86,500	16,642
Terrible! Just found out that Obama had my "wires tapped" in Trump Tower just before the victory. Nothing found. This is McCarthyism!	March 4, 2017 3:35 AM	143,915	55,070

Bill Clinton in 1994). With respect to taxes, Jason Silverstein (2017) reports:

> Data from the Organization for Economic Cooperation and Development ranks the U.S. in the middle or at the bottom of tax rates among 34 industrial nations. It had one of the lowest tax revenues by GDP percentage out of the 34 countries, and sat in the middle for tax revenue per capita and corporate tax revenue. Countries including the United Kingdom, Germany, France, Italy and Austria had far higher tax rates.

President Trump's penchant for dissembling on Twitter is not limited to communicating factual inaccuracies, however. His tweets falsely claiming that "Obama had my 'wires tapped' in Trump Tower just before the victory" and that "there was Spying in my campaign," for instance, perpetuated insidious and dangerous right-wing conspiracy theories. The latter claim, which Trump cleverly branded with the hashtag #Spygate, began when Gateway Pundit, a pro-Trump blog, published an article (Hoft, 2018), "Breaking: Senate releases unredacted texts showing FBI initiated MULTIPLE SPIES in Trump campaign in December 2015," which was picked up and tweeted by Fox Business Host Lou Dobbs and later discussed on air by Fox News host Laura Ingraham. "Between the conservative media and the president," explains Zack Beuchamp (2018), "Republican voters end up with an entirely skewed picture of reality—one in which the FBI has been plotting against Trump since December 2015." Meanwhile, Trump's abundant lies on Twitter, which include the outcome of his summit with North Korea ("There is no longer a Nuclear Threat from North Korea"), border policy ("Separating families at the Border is the fault of bad legislation passed by the Democrats"), and his motives for firing FBI Director James Comey ("I never fired James Comey because of Russia!"), sow discord and confusion, as well as undermine public trust in the institution of the press.

Distracting

In addition to using Twitter to mislead and deceive the American public, Trump regularly tweets for the purpose of distracting the public, of shifting the news away from personally damaging stories. Trump's efforts at redirecting public attention generally take one of two forms: topic shifting or blame shifting. Table 3.9 identifies ten sample tweets that illustrate these dual strategies of distraction. Among the clearest examples of topic shifting are Trump's tweets regarding football players kneeling during the national anthem. At those moments when media coverage of Trump has been particularly critical, he has raised hot-button (often racially charged) cultural issues like NFL players kneeling to shift public attention. "The NFL 'kneeling debate'," for example, "largely overshadowed the fact that 3.5 million . . . citizens face an unprecedented humanitarian crisis in Puerto Rico" (Mahafee 2017; see also Bruinius 2017). Trump's skill at topic shifting, which allows him to influence what the media and, thus, the public is talking about, is heightened by the platform of Twitter itself. Given its structural bias toward simplicity and the president's proclivity for making outrageous statements, his outrageous tweets function as ready-made headlines, headlines that, thus far, the news media has been unable to resist.

President Trump's second primary strategy of distraction on Twitter is blame shifting. In contrast to topic shifting, which aims to change *what* the news media is talking about (agenda-setting), blame shifting seeks to change *how* the news media is talking about a subject (narrative framing). Typically, blame shifting works by redirecting criticism of the president or his policies at one of his political opponents. For instance, Trump has regularly attempted to shift stories about his campaign's possible collusion with Russia and concerns over his obstruction of the Russia investigation to both former President Obama ("Since the Obama Administration was told way before the 2016 Election that the Russians were meddling why no action? Focus on them not T!") and Hillary Clinton ("So why aren't the Committees and investigators, and of course our beleaguered A.G., looking into Crooked Hillarys crimes

Table 3.9 Distracting—President Trump (Jan. 20, 2017–Sept. 1, 2018)

Tweet	Date/Time	Favorites	Retweets
Democrats are the problem. They don't care about crime and want illegal immigrants, no matter how bad they may be, to pour into and infest our Country, like MS-13. They can't win on their terrible policies, so they view them as potential voters!	June 19, 2018 6:52 AM	94,397	24,953
James Comey's Memos are Classified, I did not Declassify them. They belong to our Government! Therefore, he broke the law! Additionally, he totally made up many of the things he said I said, and he is already a proven liar and leaker. Where are Memos on Clinton, Lynch & others?	April 21, 2018 12:24 PM	76,016	20,737
So General Flynn lies to the FBI and his life is destroyed, while Crooked Hillary Clinton, on that now famous FBI holiday "interrogation" with no swearing in and no recording, lies many times . . . and nothing happens to her? Rigged system, or just a double standard?	Dec. 2, 2017 6:06 PM	139,465	41,519
Sorry, but this is years ago, before Paul Manafort was part of the Trump campaign. But why aren't Crooked Hillary & the Dems the focus?????	Oct. 30, 2017 7:25 AM	118,225	33,616
All of this "Russia" talk right when the Republicans are making their big push for historic Tax Cuts & Reform. Is this coincidental? NOT!	Oct. 29, 2017 7:48 AM	90,835	22,787
The issue of kneeling has nothing to do with race. It is about respect for our Country Flag and National Anthem. NFL must respect this!	Sept. 25, 2017 4:39 AM	200,643	53,579
So why aren't the Committees and investigators, and of course our beleaguered A.G., looking into Crooked Hillarys crimes & Russia relations?	July 24, 2017 5:49 AM	84,321	23,880
Since the Obama Administration was told way before the 2016 Election that the Russians were meddling why no action? Focus on them not T!	June 24, 2017 1:28 PM	84,767	20,462
Crooked H destroyed phones w/ hammer, 'bleached' emails, & had husband meet w/AG days before she was cleared-& they talk about obstruction?	June 15, 2017 12:56 PM	145,891	51,181
Just out: The same Russian Ambassador that met Jeff Sessions visited the Obama White House 22 times and 4 times last year alone.	March 4 2017 3:42 AM	115,495	35,676

& Russia relations?" and "Crooked H destroyed phones w/ hammer, 'bleached' emails, & had husband meet w/AG days before she was cleared-& they talk about obstruction?"). Similarly, he has suggested that negative news narratives about General Flynn, James Comey, and Paul Manafort should all be about Hillary Clinton. Trump's favorite objects of blame (i.e., scapegoats) since being elected president are Hillary Clinton (128 tweets), Barak Obama (212 tweets), and the Democrats (262 tweets). In trying to shift attention away from his administration's monstrous policy of separating children from their parents at the border, he both tried to blame Democrats and to dehumanize immigrants by implicitly comparing them to pests or rodents ("illegal immigrants . . . pour into and infest our Country").

Discrediting

This category of tweets involves Trump's efforts to attack and disparage his critics; specifically, it seeks to discredit them by challenging their honesty and integrity. The two primary targets of Trump's discrediting tweets are the mainstream news media, especially CNN, NBC, and the *New York Times*, and the Federal Bureau of Investigation (FBI) and the US Department of Justice (DOJ), especially former FBI Director James Comey, special counsel Robert Mueller, and Attorney General Jeff Sessions. Like other authoritarians throughout history and around the globe, a central feature of President Trump's rhetoric is his attack of a free and independent press. In an off-camera discussion with *60 Minutes* reporter Lesley Stahl, Trump admitted that he routinely bashes journalists "to discredit you all and demean you all so that when you write negative stories about me no one will believe you" (quoted in Mangan 2018). He, of course, does not bash all journalists or news outlets, only those that are critical of him, which he effectively announced in a threatening tweet on May 9, 2018:

> The Fake News is working overtime. Just reported that, despite the tremendous success we are having with the economy & all things else, 91% of the Network News about me is negative (Fake). Why do we work so hard in working with the media when it is corrupt? Take away credentials?
>
> (Quoted in Lind 2018)

Trump's Twitter attacks on journalists and media outlets who have been critical of him are alarming, especially when he frames those outlets as "enemies of the American people!" and "Our Country's biggest enemy," as he did on multiple occasions in 2017 and 2018.

This language echoes the phrase *vrag naroda* ("enemy of the people"), which Lenin and Stalin employed to attack opposition from intellectuals, clergy, and others to the Bolshevik movement. Equally troubling are Trump's frequent attacks on law-enforcement officials, agencies, and the judicial branch of government. Several of the tweets in Table 3.10 show that Trump, in his rhetorical efforts to discredit the Russia investigation, regularly accuses those associated with the investigation as being unethical or, worse, as being guilty of crimes ("[Comey] illegally leaked CLASSIFIED INFORMATION" and "Mueller probe . . . was based on fraudulent activities and a Fake Dossier paid for by Crooked Hillary and the DNC, and improperly used in FISA COURT for surveillance of my campaign"). And though we have not included any examples in our table, Trump routinely criticizes judges who have ruled against him in court cases. In short, his tweets demonstrate a general disregard for the US justice system and the rule of law. For Trump followers, however, discrediting tweets function to affirm the perception that Trump is treated unkindly and unfairly.

Table 3.10 Discrediting—President Trump (Jan. 20, 2017–Sept. 1, 2018)

Tweet	Date/ Time	Favorites	Retweets
So funny to watch the Fake News, especially NBC and CNN. They are fighting hard to downplay the deal with North Korea. 500 days ago they would have "begged" for this deal-looked like war would break out. Our Country's biggest enemy is the Fake News so easily promulgated by fools!	June 13, 2018 6:30 AM	162,322	42,544
When and where will all of the many conflicts of interest be listed by the 13 Angry Democrats (plus) working on the Witch Hunt Hoax. There has never been a group of people on a case so biased or conflicted. It is all a Democrat Excuse for LOSING the Election. Where is the server?	June 7, 2018 6:07 AM	72,497	17,975
Is everybody believing what is going on. James Comey can't define what a leak is. He illegally leaked CLASSIFIED INFORMATION but doesn't understand what he did or how serious it is. He lied all over the place to cover it up. He's either very sick or very dumb. Remember sailor!	April 27, 2018 3:26 AM	107,626	24,791

Table 3.10 (Continued)

Tweet	Date/ Time	Favorites	Retweets
DOJ just issued the McCabe report—which is a total disaster. He LIED! LIED! LIED! McCabe was totally controlled by Comey— McCabe is Comey!! No collusion all made up by this den of thieves and lowlifes!	April 13, 2018 12:36 PM	126,103	36,163
The Mueller probe should never have been started in that there was no collusion and there was no crime. It was based on fraudu-lent activities and a Fake Dossier paid for by Crooked Hillary and the DNC, and improperly used in FISA COURT for sur-veillance of my campaign. WITCH HUNT!	March 17, 2018 5:12 PM	102,780	28,841
Little Adam Schiff who is desperate to run for higher office is one of the biggest liars and leakers in Washington right up there with Comey Warner Brennan and Clapper! Adam leaves closed committee hearings to illegally leak confidential information. Must be stopped!	Feb. 5, 2018 4:39 AM	139,352	41,801
How can FBI Deputy Director Andrew McCabe, the man in charge, along with leakin' James Comey, of the Phony Hillary Clinton investigation (including her 33000 illegally deleted emails) be given $700000 for wife's campaign by Clinton Puppets during investigation?	Dec. 23, 2017 12:27 PM	119,983	35,521
CNN'S slogan is CNN, THE MOST TRUSTED NAME IN NEWS. Everyone knows this is not true, that this could, in fact, be a fraud on the American Public. There are many outlets that are far more trusted than Fake News CNN. Their slogan should be CNN, THE LEAST TRUSTED NAME IN NEWS!	Dec. 9, 2017 5:21 AM	143,115	35,464
The ABC/Washington Post Poll, even though almost 40% is not bad at this time, was just about the most inaccurate poll around election time!	July 16, 2017 7:10 AM	69,426	13,374
The FAKE NEWS media (failing @nytimes, @NBCNews, @ABC, @CBS, @CNN) is not my enemy, it is the enemy of the American People!	Feb. 17, 2017 1:48 PM	155,296	50,546

Implications and Conclusion

In his 1985 bestselling book *Amusing Ourselves to Death: Public Discourse in the Age of Show Business*, influential cultural critic and media ecologist Neil Postman argued that the ubiquity of television had substantially undermined the quality of public discourse in America. Upon first reading Postman's book, his argument can seem reductionistic. He appears, after all, to be condemning an entire medium of communication on the basis that it promoted a different way of processing information than print-based media. But Postman's claim was considerably more nuanced than that. He was not, in fact, denouncing all television. On the contrary, Postman was quite clear that he had no objection to "television's junk," noting that, "The best things on television *are* its junk, and no one and nothing is seriously threatened by it" (p. 16). What did concern Postman was when television aspired to be more than junk, when it presented "itself as a carrier of important cultural conversations" (p. 16), when political, religious, and educational discourse was filtered through television.

In the more than 30 years since the publication of the first edition of *Amusing Ourselves to Death*, Postman's argument has become all the more compelling, not least of all because society is going through another paradigmatic change, a fundamental shift in the dominant mode of communication. Just as the Age of Typography gave way to Age of Television, the Age of Television has steadily given way to the Age of Twitter.[1] Like all communication revolutions, the rise of Twitter, along with other social media, does not signal the end or disappearance of older media like television. Emerging media do, however, transform existing media. So, while Twitter had a "largely symbiotic relationship with television . . . particularly as a cross-promotion platform" (Brouder and Brookey 2015, p. 46) in its early years, over time it has transformed our televisual landscape and, consequently, the character of our public discourse. Whereas television produced public discourse that was silly, ridiculous, and impotent, Twitter produces public discourse that is simple, impetuous, and uncivil. Twitter and other social media platforms work to undermine complex, considered, and compassionate communication, thereby, contributing to the divisive and coarsening tone of political discourse in the United States.

Nowhere is this more evident than in the communication style and behavior of Twitter's most infamous user, President Donald Trump. While Trump's tweeting has evolved somewhat over time, shifting from a focus on self-promoting an image of business success to the tactical use of the platform to position himself as an

Table 3.11 Alignment of Trump's Twitter use with the platform's defining traits

Traits of Twitter	Citizen Trump	Candidate Trump	President Trump
Simplicity	Branding	Defining	Dissembling
Impulsivity	Boasting	Disrupting	Distracting
Incivility	Bullying	Demeaning	Discrediting

anti-establishment candidate to its strategic implementation to support a distorted, narcissistic worldview, it has consistently reflected and reinforced the underlying structural logic of Twitter. Indeed, as Table 3.11 highlights, Trump's central rhetorical aims in each of the contexts examined (citizen, candidate, and president) align closely with the platform's defining traits.

Whether employing Twitter to *brand* his products and properties, to *define* "Make America Great Again," or to *dissemble* reality, Trump has mastered the art of the short, simple message. Further, his compulsion to say whatever he is thinking at any given moment—*boasting* about successes both real and imagined, *disrupting* social and political norms, and *distracting* from unflattering news with shocking or scandalous statements—stems from his impulsive behavior. Finally, his tendency to *bully*, *demean*, and *discredit* others reflects the platform's bias toward incivility. To these three underlying properties of Twitter, Trump has added a four crucial trait: repetition.

In addition to tweeting simple, impulsive, and uncivil messages, Trump repeats them endlessly. Since the presidential election, Trump has—as of this writing (December 10, 2018)—referred to the Russia investigation on Twitter as a "witch hunt" 147 times, and more than half of those mentions were in three months alone. He has tweeted critically about James Comey 104 times, about the FBI 166 times, and about the "fake news" media 311 times. Trump has even demonstrated a willingness to attack special counsel Robert Mueller directly, tweeting about him 67 times since March 2018. Alarmingly, data suggest that such attacks have been effective, especially among Trump's followers, who are inclined to believe him. A Politico/Morning Consult Poll of June 13, 2018, for instance, found that Mueller had a 53 percent unfavorable rating among Republications. "Up from 27 percent in July 2017," Jen Kirby described the poll as, "an unsettlingly sign that the president's attacks on the special counsel—bolstered by conservative media—are having an effect" (Kirby 2018). The "Trump Effect," Trump's ability to shape public opinion through Twitter and the Fox News echo chamber, is also evident in attitudes toward the news media; one poll found that 92 percent of Republicans believe "traditional news outlets knowingly report false or misleading stories at least sometimes" (Fischer 2018). Even more terrifyingly, 78 percent of Republicans believe they can spot fake news.

The research, however, suggests otherwise. Kai Shu et al. (2017) found that not only are most consumers of fake news unable to identify it, but also that exposure to "fake news changes the way people interpret and respond to real news . . . . impeding their abilities to differentiate what is true from what is not" (p. 22). The problems associated with fake news are made even more challenging by the fact that 62 percent of US adults get their news on social media outlets like Twitter (Gottfried and Shearer 2016). Such outlets regularly feature fake and misleading stories from sources devoid of editorial standards. Moreover, users are targeted based on their political proclivities (i.e., what items they "like," which sites they visit, and whom they are "friends" with). In short, people are fed a steady diet of what they want to hear in social media contexts. The result is the creation of ideological silos, powerful echo chambers of misinformation that, thanks to confirmation bias, reaffirm existing beliefs (Solon 2016). For many Americans, their primary political involvement during the 2016 election cycle was limited to tweeting and retweeting snarky anti-Clinton or anti-Trump memes to like-minded individuals (i.e., "followers"), or posting and liking links to articles on Facebook that reflected their political leanings. These activities, however, do not foster reasoned public deliberation among people of diverse backgrounds and experiences; they produce an uninformed, uncritical, and irresponsible electorate. And it is that electorate that Trump has masterfully manipulated on Twitter, a platform that was ready-made for his simple-minded views, reckless behavior, and hateful rhetoric.

Note

1. We're calling it the "Age of Twitter" for parallelism with the Age of Typography and the Age of Television, but the Age of Twitter is really the Age of Social Media.

References

Abravanel, L. 2012. @piersmorgan when he says 'many', he means the voices in his overinflated, inexplicably coiffed head, right? [Twitter]. November 10. Available at: twitter.com/realdonaldtrump/status/267286471172562944?lang=en [Accessed August 20, 2018].

Beuchamp, Z. 2018. Trump, Fox News, and Twitter have created a dangerous conspiracy theory loop. *Vox* [online]. Available at: www.vox.com/world/2018/6/6/17433876/trump-spygate-fox-twitter [Accessed July 7, 2018].

Biggs, T. 2016. Donald Trump Twitter-bot is hilarious and terrifyingly real. *The Sydney Morning Herald* [online]. Available at: www.smh.com.au/technology/innovation/donald-trump-twitterbot-is-hilarious-and-terrifyingly-real-20160308-gne1ya.html [Accessed August 20, 2018].

Bilton, N. 2016. Trump's biggest lie? The size of his Twitter following. *Vanity Fair* [online]. Available at: www.vanityfair.com/news/2016/08/trumps-biggest-lie-the-size-of-his-%20twitter-following [Accessed August 20, 2018].

Brouder, M. and Brookey, R. A. 2015. Twitter and television: Broadcast ratings in the web 2.0 era. In: J. V. Pavlik, ed. *Digital technology and the future of broadcasting: Global perspectives.* New York: Routledge, pp. 45–59.

Bruinius, H. 2017. With NFL controversy, did media play into Trump's 'distraction tactics'? *The Christian Science Monitor* [online]. Available at: www.csmonitor.com/USA/Politics/2017/0928/With-NFL-controversy-did-media-play-into-Trump-s-distraction-tactics [Accessed February 19, 2018].

Burke, K. 1984. *Permanence and change: An anatomy of purpose*, 3rd ed. Berkeley: University of California Press.

Carr, N. 2010. *The shallows: What the internet is doing to our brains.* New York: W. W. Norton & Company.

Carr, N. 2018. Why Trump tweets (and why we listen). *Politico* [online]. Available at: www.politico.com/magazine/story/2018/01/26/donald-trump-twitter-addiction-216530 [Accessed July 5, 2018].

De Certeau, M. 1984. *Practice of everyday life*, translated by S. Randall. Berkeley: University of California Press.

Enli, G. 2017. Twitter as arena for the authentic outsider: Exploring the social media campaigns of Trump and Clinton in the 2016 US presidential election. *European Journal of Communication*, 32(1), pp. 50–61.

Fischer, S. 2018. Trump effect: most republicans think news outlets report fake news. *Axios* [online]. Available at: www.axios.com/trump-effect-92-percent-republicans-media-fake-news-9c1bbf70-0054-41dd-b506-0869bb10f08c.html [Accessed 30 June 2018].

Gabler, N. 2016. Donald Trump, the emperor of social media. *Moyers & Company* [online]. Available at: billmoyers.com/story/donald-trump-the-emperor-of-social-media/[Accessed August 20, 2018].

Gottfried, J., and Shearer, E. 2016 News use across social media platforms 2016. *PewResearchCenter* [online]. Available at: www.journalism.org/2016/05/26/news-use-across-social-media-platforms-2016/ [Accessed 20 June 2017].

Heffernan, V. 2016. How the Twitter candidate trumped the teleprompter President. *Politico* [online]. Available at: www.politico.com/magazine/story/2016/04/2016-heffernan-twitter-media-donald-trump-barack-obama-teleprompter-president-213825 [Accessed August 19, 2018].

Hoft, J. 2018. Breaking: Senate releases unredacted Strzok—Page texts showing FBI initiated multiple spies in Trump Campaign in December 2015. *Gateway*

Pundit [online]. Available at: www.thegatewaypundit.com/2018/06/breaking-senate-releases-unredacted-strzok-page-texts-showing-fbi-initiated-multiple-spies-in-trump-campaign-in-december-2015/ [Accessed 1 August 2018].

Kapko, M. 2016. Twitter's impact on 2016 presidential election is unmistakable. *CIO* [online]. Available at: www.cio.com/article/3137513/social-networking/twitters-impact-on-2016-presidential-election-is-unmistakable.html [Accessed August 20, 2018].

Kirby, J. 2018. Poll: Only 32 percent of voters view Robert Mueller favorably. *Vox* [online]. Available at: www.vox.com/2018/6/13/17460046/robert-mueller-trump-russia-poll [Accessed June 29 2018].

Lind, D. 2018. President Donald Trump finally admits that "fake news" just means news he doesn't like. *Vox* [online]. Available at:www.vox.com/policy-and-politics/2018/5/9/17335306/trump-tweet-twitter-latest-fake-news-credentials [Accessed 12 June 2018].

Loh, K. K. and Kanai, R. 2015. How has the internet reshaped human cognition? *The Neuroscientist* [online]. Available at:www.ncbi.nlm.nih.gov/pubmed/26170005 [Accessed March 15, 2017].

Mahaffee, D. 2017. Trump's tweets distract us from America's pressing challenges. *The Hill* [online]. Available at: thehill.com/opinion/white-house/352666-trumps-tweets-distract-us-from-americas-pressing-challenges [Accessed December 22, 2017].

Mangan, D. 2018. President Trump told Lesley Stahl he bashes press 'to demean you and discredit you so . . . no one will believe' negative stories about him. *CNBC* [online]. Available at: www.cnbc.com/2018/05/22/trump-told-lesley-stahl-he-bashes-press-to-discredit-negative-stories.html [Accessed June 17, 2018].

Merrill, J. B. 2015. How Donald Trump talks. *New York Times* [online]. Available at: www.nytimes.com/interactive/2015/12/05/us/politics/donald-trump-talk.html?_r=1 [Accessed August 20, 2018].

Meyrowitz, J. 1994. Medium theory. In: D. Crowley and D. Mitchell, eds. *Communication theory today*. Stanford: Stanford University Press, pp. 50–77.

Naaman, M., Boase, J., and Lai, C.-K. 2010. Is it really about me? Message content in social awareness streams. In: K. Inkpen and C. Gutwin, eds. *Proceedings of the 2010 ACM conference on computer supported cooperative work*. New York: ACM Press, pp. 189–192.

Petersen, J. 2016. Trump's Twitter followed by millions of inactive or fake accounts. *The Washington Free Beacon* [online]. Available at: freebeacon.com/politics/trumps-twitter-followed-millions-inactive-fake-accounts/ [Accessed August 20, 2018]

Postman, N. 1985. *Amusing ourselves to death: Public discourse in the age of show business*. New York: Penguin Books.

Shafer, J. 2015. Donald Trump talks like a third grader. *Politico* [online]. Available at: www.politico.com/magazine/story/2015/08/donald-trump-talks-like-a-third-grader-121340 [Accessed August 20, 2018].

Schu, K. et al. 2017. Fake news detection on social media: A data mining perspective. *ACM SIGKDD Explorations Newsletter*, 19(1), pp. 22–36.

Silverstein, J. 2017. President Trump promotes his tax plan by tweeting major falsehood about America's taxes. *New York Daily News* [online]. Available at: www.nydailynews.com/news/politics/trump-promotes-tax-plan-major-falsehood-u-s-taxes-article-1.3473726 [Accessed June 14, 2018].

Solon, O. 2016. Facebook's failure: Did fake news and polarized politics get Trump elected? *Guardian* [online]. Available at: www.theguardian.com/technology/2016/nov/10/facebook-fake-news-election-conspiracy-theories?CMP = oth_b-aplnews_d-1 [Accessed July 22, 2017].

Sosis, J. 2012. @realDonaldTrump You're not even the best 140 character writer in your car right now. Shut your trap you waste of life. [Twitter]. November 10. Available at: twitter.com/realdonaldtrump/status/26728647 1172562944?lang=en [Accessed August 20, 2018].

Spellman, J. 2012. FYI "Many" is twitter slang for "No one" @realDonaldTrump Many are saying I'm the best 140 character writer in the world. [Twitter]. November 10. Available at: twitter.com/realdonaldtrump/status/2672864711 72562944?lang=en [Accessed August 20, 2018].

Stieglitz, S. and Dang-Xuan, L. 2013. Emotions and information diffusion in social media—sentiment of microblogs and sharing behavior. *Journal of Management Information Systems* 29(4), pp. 217–247.

Sullivan, A. 2018. Trump is making us all live in his delusional reality show. *New York Magazine* [online]. Available at: nymag.com/daily/intelligencer/2018/06/trump-is-making-us-all-live-in-his-delusional-reality-show.html [Accessed August 3, 2018].

Sumner, C. et al. 2012. Predicting dark triad personality traits from Twitter usage and a linguistic analysis of tweets. *11th International Conference on Machine Learning and Applications (ICMLA)*, 2, pp. 386–393.

Sweeney, J. 2016. I can't imagine how stressed Americans are feeling right now. I'm Canadian and I'm chugging maple syrup and just punched a moose. [Twitter]. November 8. Available at: twitter.com/sween/status/796 172430641393664?lang=en [Accessed August 5, 2018].

Tait, A. 2016. The strange case of Marina Joyce and internet hysteria. *Guardian* [online]. Available at: www.theguardian.com/technology/2016/aug/04/marina-joyce-internet-hysteria-witch-hunts-cyberspace [Accessed August 20, 2018].

Thelwall, M., Buckley, K., and Paltoglou, G. 2011. Sentiment in Twitter events. *Journal of the American Society for Information Science and Technology*, 62(2), pp. 406–418.

Trump, D. J. 2012. Thanks-many are saying I'm the best 140 character writer in the world. It's easy when it's fun. [Twitter]. November 10. Available at: twitter.com/realdonaldtrump/status/267286471172562944?lang=en [Accessed May 13, 2018].

Trump, D. J. 2018. As has been stated by numerous legal scholars, I have the absolute right to PARDON myself, but why would I do that when I have done nothing wrong? [Twitter] June 4. Available at: twitter.com/realdonaldtrump/status/1003616210922147841?lang=en [Accessed July 10, 2018].

Tumulty, K. 2017. How Donald Trump came up with 'make America great again.' *The Washington Post* [online]. Available at: www.washington-post.com/politics/how-donald-trump-came-up-with-make-america-great-again/2017/01/17/fb6acf5e-dbf7–11e6-ad42-f3375f271c9c_story.html?po stshare=831484737469175&utm_term=.b5f288bc7f65 [Accessed January 12, 2018].

Zubiaga, A. et. al. 2015. Real-time classification of Twitter trends. *Journal of the Association for Information Science and Technology*, 66(3), pp. 462–373.

4 In Defense of Democracy

Donald Trump poses an unusual challenge to critics because his rhetoric does not reflect a consistent policy platform or a coherent ideological position. As such, we have argued that Trump's rhetorical appeal is best understood neither through substantive analysis nor ideological critique. Rather, Trump's rhetoric is best approached through the lens of style, the aesthetic expression of a shared cultural sentiment or sensibility. Throughout this book, we have demonstrated that Trump performs an emergent populist style of "white rage," whose affects are widely diffused through the social media platform of Twitter. Trump's rhetorical style is so effective because of the unique way it combines his general manner of speaking with his preferred modality of speaking. Operating principally on an affective register, white rage entails pride in explicit demonstrations of white male privilege, and anger and resentment at anything and anyone regarded as subverting that privilege. Twitter—with its characteristics of simplicity, impulsivity, and incivility—is the perfect vehicle to carry this message.

Though Donald Trump did not manufacture white rage, he most assuredly mainstreamed it (Cose 2018). Early in the primaries, it was evident that Trump's base supporters were disaffected working-class whites who feared "a reduction in the unearned material advantages that come as a result of white [male] privilege" (Devega 2016a) Post-election polling confirms this; it found that racial resentment and anti-immigrant attitudes were among the best predictors, comparable to partisan identification (Republican vs. Democrat), of whether or not a white voter supported Trump (McElwee and McDaniel 2017). Religion was also a strong predictor of support; winning 81 percent of the white evangelical vote, conservative Christians backed Trump in higher numbers than George W. Bush, John McCain, and Mitt Romney (Posner 2017). As one commentator has speculated, evangelicals, both men and women, gravitated to Trump—despite his obvious

irreligiosity and demonstrated moral deficiencies—because he represented "the possibility of a return to patriarchy, to a time when men
were men, and didn't have to apologize for it" (Foer 2016).[1]

Donald Trump won the 2016 election in large measure by tapping
into extant fears and anxieties associated with "the slow-declining
supremacy of white men in the U.S." (Cauterucci 2017). He stoked and
mobilized these fears, not by making rational arguments or proposing
convincing policy reforms, but by mirroring the anger and resentment
of his followers, by concentrating and reflecting it back to them. Donald Trump is the walking, talking embodiment of white rage, which he
enacts through his authoritarian management style, bullying manner,
and hyperbolic, narcissistic, and demagogic discourse. Moreover, his
preferred outlet for the performance of this rhetorical manner is Twitter,
a social media platform whose structural characteristics lend themselves
to the transmission of affect generally and negative affect specifically.
The affective spread of white rage has demonstrated remarkable sway
among Trump's followers, who continue to back him regardless of his
obvious lies, apparent corruption, and potential collusion with Russia.

Trump's followers do not care if his campaign conspired with a foreign
power to influence the election; they do not care if the president or his
campaign attempted to obstruct investigators from finding out if such
collusion occurred; they do not care about the standing of the US on the
world stage; they do not—as it turns out—even care if the president pur-
sues and implements policies that improve their lives. They care only that
liberals, minorities, and foreigners were "put in their place" by Trump's
election (Marcotte 2016). Prior to the election, 81 percent of Trump's
supporters reported that life had gotten worse for "people like them"
in the last 50 years. In May 2017, when his supporters were asked that
same question, only 41 percent said it had gotten worse (Edwards-Levy
2017). Apparently, the election of a president who routinely expresses
racist, sexist, and xenophobic views was itself sufficient for Trump followers to feel more optimistic. But what lessons can be gleaned from the
preceding analysis? To answer this question, we undertake two goals in
the conclusion: to highlight the material consequentiality of Trump's
rhetorical style and to discuss how we might foster and promote a more
democratic and progressive politics going forward.

The Consequentiality of Trump's Rhetoric

Our analysis of the manner and mode of Donald Trump's rhetoric suggests six main consequences of the president's enactment of white rage
and his repeated use of Twitter as the primary platform by which to

express his personal opinions and communicate his grievances. Specifically, we contend that President Trump's rhetoric: (1) undermines civility and degrades the level of political discourse in the US; (2) erodes democratic norms and institutions; (3) weakens the rule of law; (4) fuels racial hatred and fosters discrimination and violence; (5) favors anti-intellectualism and undermines critical thought; and (6) promotes mistrust of the mainstream news media and facilitates a post-truth politics.

1. *Civility and political discourse.* As the preceding analysis demonstrates, part of Trump's appeal was his flouting of social decorum, which his voters associate with a culture of political correctness and, worse, "liberalism." The president's consistently crude and indecorous discourse, especially his penchant for dehumanizing rhetoric and name-calling on Twitter, has emboldened others to speak and act in similar ways. When the president refers to former White House staffer Omarosa Manigault Newman as a "dog" on Twitter, he demeans the office of the president and implicitly endorses such discourse. The president's frequent use of degrading and dehumanizing rhetoric not only contributes to an increasing incivility in our politics, but it also encourages physical violence. Trump's election, for instance, corresponds to an uptick in both anti-abortion vitriol and violence. While anti-abortion harassment and terrorism typically decline during Republican administrations, "In the first five months of 2017, [there were] four times as many online threats and death wishes directed at abortion providers compared with the same period in 2016" (Goldberg 2017).

2. *Democratic norms and institutions.* While Trump's attacks on a free and independent press are well known, he has assaulted the freedom of expression more generally. In the closing days of the 2016 presidential campaign, for instance, Trump accused *Saturday Night Live* of doing a "hit job on me," railed against the show as "terrible" on Twitter, and demanded its cancellation. Since his election, Trump has attacked female comedians Michelle Wolff and Samantha Bee for being critical of him and his administration. In the case of Wolff, he suggested that the annual White House Correspondents' Dinner, which he refused to attend, be terminated, tweeting "The filthy 'comedian' totally bombed. Put Dinner to rest or start over." In the instance of Bee, Trump called for her firing, tweeting, "Why aren't they firing no talent Samantha Bee for the horrible language used on her low ratings show? A total double standard." Much like the dictators he so admires, Trump is intolerant of any speech criticizing him and he actively seeks to harm those who speak out against him (Obeidallah 2018).

3. *The rule of law.* As CNN legal analyst Joan Biskupic wrote in May 2018:

> Over the past 24 months, Trump has scorned judges, derided the American court system, and trampled on all manner of constitutional principles. Trump has especially ridiculed due process of the law, the bedrock against government's arbitrary denial of a person's life, liberty or property.
>
> (Biskupic 2018)

Trump clearly signaled his contempt for the rule of law, as well as his racism, during the campaign when he critiqued US District Court Judge Gonzalo Curiel, who was presiding over a lawsuit against Trump University, for his "Mexican" heritage. In office, Trump has spoken in favor of summary deportations at the border (even for immigrants seeking political asylum), suggested that NFL players who refuse to kneel during the Star-Spangled Banner "shouldn't be in the country," and called—repeatedly—for the investigation and imprisonment of his defeated political opponent: Hillary Clinton (Biskupic 2018). Moreover, as *Slate* reported in August 2018, the Trump administration is seeking "to strip Americans who were simply born and raised near the border with Mexico of their citizenship" (Hannon 2018).

4. *Racial hatred and discrimination.* From Trump's comments following the white supremacist march in Charlottesville in August 2017 to his retweeting of an anti-Muslim propaganda video in November 2017, the president has consistently employed racist rhetoric. As Carolyn Bernucca notes:

> If there is one thing that the president consistently outdoes himself on, it's offending marginalized people. . . . no one has been safe from President Donald Trump's discriminatory language. Women, Mexicans, Muslims, black people, and people with disabilities were all subjected to hate as he rallied supporters—and since his win, things have only gotten worse.
>
> (Bernucca 2017)

The president's unapologetic and openly racist rhetoric has prompted others to respond in kind. One study "shows that the election liberated people to express feelings they'd otherwise keep to themselves" (Sunstein 2017). As of July 2017, the number of confirmed incidents this year of "white students using Trump's words and slogans to bully classmates" stood at 81 (Samaha 2017). But Trump's hateful rhetoric has done more than merely invite imitation from his followers; it has contributed to a culture of violence against minorities, as evidenced by the sharp rise in hate crimes following his election (Grewal 2018; NCAAP 2018).

5. *Anti-intellectualism.* Trump's insistence on communicating with the American public principally through the modality of Twitter is central to the way his rhetoric favors anti-intellectualism and undermines critical thought. As we discussed in Chapter 3, the defining structural features of Twitter disallow sophisticated messaging. Consequently, in tweeting, the president offers decidedly simplistic views on complex political issues and topics, an effect that is magnified by the simplicity and low readability level of Trump's language (Kayam 2018). The president's claim that "trade wars are good, and easy to win," for instance, not only betrays his fundamental economic ignorance, but also reduces the multidimensional issue of trade to the polarities of winning and losing. Trump further contributes to the trend of anti-intellectualism through his discursive distain for science, facts, knowledge, expertise, and common sense. Given the extreme narcissistic character of his rhetoric, Trump's *opinion*s and *feelings* matter above all else to his policy positions and beliefs. Like Trump, his followers are proud of their ignorance and despise experts and expertise (Decker 2017).

6. *Post-truth politics.* Trump is fostering a dangerous, conspiracy-minded, fact-indifferent sensibility among a significant segment of the American electorate. He is doing this principally through his attacks on the mainstream news media as "fake news" and the "enemy of the people." Increasingly, Trump's followers have begun to distrust the reporting of credible and conscientious news organizations. While the president (mis)uses the phrase "fake news" to refer to reporting that is unfavorable to him, "fake news" describes an actual phenomenon, which is: (1) the generation of information deliberately designed to mislead consumers and (2) packaged to resemble reliable and trustworthy journalism. While CNN, MSNBC, and the *New York Times* occasionally make errors in their reporting, they quickly correct them. This is not fake news. Fake news, for instance, is the concerted effort of the Russian government to flood social media sites with intentionally false and misleading information during the 2016 presidential campaign. That Trump's followers do not understand or appreciate this fundamental distinction is among the most serious threats posed by Trump's rhetoric.

Toward an Affective Politics of Resistance

Despite these truly alarming implications, there remains some basis for hope or, at the very least, opportunity. The preceding analysis is grounded in the idea that individual and social bodies have histories and tendencies. Trump's style was affectively appealing precisely because it was not really *his* style, but a much more widely felt cultural sensibility among largely white male voters. What Trump did was become a focal point of that sensibility, exciting and charging it across a network of bodies much as an electric spark might ignite a fire. But even as he did that, he produced a counter-spark among bodies with different histories and tendencies, and the cultural sensibility at work there, in contrast to white rage, might be termed "reasonable disgust," and it seems to be spreading and intensifying. Unlike rage, which is a negatively oriented affect (concerned *only* with rejection), disgust is more ambivalent (Tomkins 1995, p. 84). Having evolved from the basic instinct for self-preservation, disgust protects us against toxic elements in our environment. It is an abrupt halting, a warning to alter course, a temporary suspension that requires a subsequent course of action. So, while disgust *begins* with rejection (of toxins), it is an energy that can be harnessed to move in a new direction. As such, disgust can serve negative or positive ends depending upon what follows from it.

In the remainder of the conclusion, we examine how disgust might be mobilized in the service of a progressive politics by coupling it with love rather than anger. The importance of style, and by extension affect, both to Trump's political success and to the possibilities for resistance is crucial in this regard.

As scholars of rhetoric, we must be careful not to equate Trump's political success, or the success of any politician for that matter, too strongly with the actions of an individual agent. Trump is not some rhetorical genius who masterminded a clever, new political strategy. All available evidence indicates that Trump's success was not strategic (i.e., carefully planned and thoughtfully executed), and that he has never successfully masterminded anything. Trump's performance of white rage "worked" not because he is a skilled politician or businessman (clearly he is neither), but because he offered a compelling expression of an already existing cultural sensibility. By openly enacting white male privilege, along with anger at its decentering, Trump exploited that sensibility for personal gain (he is plainly self-interested). But since Trump did not create this sensibility, any serious attempt to combat Trump must begin by combatting that sensibility.

Toward this end, and this is the second implication of the preceding analysis, rhetorical scholars must look beyond reason and, consequently, ideology as the sole or even primary basis for understanding the appeal of rhetoric. White rage is not a coherent set of ideas and beliefs, but an intensely felt public sentiment. It is expressed aesthetically and experienced affectively. As such, progressives cannot combat it exclusively or perhaps even primarily with alternative ideas advanced via rational argument. The political Left is simply not going to persuade with logic disaffected working-class whites who feel threatened and left behind. Trump's base supporters are, by most accounts, uninterested in and uncompelled by fact-based arguments, but they are, according to neuroscientific research, especially prone to "feelings of fear and disgust" (Devega 2016b). Trump has already excited and capitalized on their fears of the racial Other. If progressives hope to combat this, they will need to mobilize other powerful and structurally engaged public affects.

We might, for instance, mobilize our deeply felt disgust, and there is certainly plenty to be reasonably disgusted about. Disgust is an affect we often feel when confronted by injustice. When someone does us wrong, misunderstanding our core being, or limiting our life choices, we are justifiably disgusted. When we see, for example, young children stripped from their parents at the US/Mexico border we are disgusted. Many of us are disgusted on behalf of the family, for they have been treated with deeply dehumanizing injustice. But we are also disgusted on our own behalf, for we see that the country to which we pledge allegiance is carrying out that injustice in our name. This, we know deep in our souls, does not make America great. Such actions profoundly misunderstand who many of us are.

While disgust is a reasonable affective response to the racism, misogyny, homophobia, and xenophobia of our present moment, it must be combined with something else if we hope to mobilize it for progressive purposes. Ultimately, we must decide what to do with our disgust, to allow it to simmer and turn into anger and even rage, or to turn, instead, toward love. For Americans who felt aggrieved by the decentering of white masculinity, they confronted a similar choice. Many, like President Trump, opted for rage, an affect that, to them, feels justified. To the extent that anti-racism attempts to undo structures that have secured white privilege for 500 years, and anti-misogyny contests structures that have secured male privilege for centuries, such challenges to the status quo felt threatening. White rage has been one response to this felt threat. But it is a decidedly divisive response. As Kenneth Burke would point out, this is a tragic frame wherein one responds to a perceived injustice with an effort to identify and destroy enemies, and in which one's anger must be purer, more powerful, and more effective (Burke 1937). Alternatively, it is possible when confronted with disgust to choose love over anger, to choose affiliative rather than divisive affects.

We can choose in the face of reasonable disgust to respond with affiliative affects and, in fact, we would argue we must. We must tap into affects that do not narrow the number of those who we are with, nor purify the identities that count as good. Indeed, we must find a way of feeling connected that—to use Burke's language again—transcends the tragedy of us and them (Burke 1937). We offer the public affects of love and hope and generosity. These too have deep histories and are woven into the US American experience. James Baldwin (1993), writing in the still important *The Fire Next Time*, puts love at the center of an anti-racist project. More recently George Yancy (2015) also features love asking white America to "*listen with love*. Well at least try*,*" while Michael Eric Dyson (2017) returns again and again to a difficult kind of love in *Tears We Cannot Stop*.

Love may seem misaligned with our claims about the deep and embedded nature of racism. After all, racism—as with misogyny, homophobia, and xenophobia—is structural; it is linked to amassing and dispersing material goods. Love, by contrast, seems rather more personal and individual. But for Baldwin, love is also deeply woven into our history. Crucially, love exists, "not merely in the personal sense but as a state of being, or a state of grace—not in the infantile American sense of being made happy but in the tough and universal sense of quest and daring and growth" (Baldwin 1993, p. 95). Whiteness, he argues, is marked by a profound lovelessness, an inability to feel with and for others. Near the end of *The Fire Next Time* (1993), he writes:

> All of us know, whether or not we are able to admit it, that mirrors can only lie, that death by drowning is all that awaits one there. It is for this reason that love is so desperately sought and so cunningly avoided. Love takes off the masks that we fear we cannot live without and know we cannot live within.
>
> (p. 95)

Without love, whiteness cannot imagine intimacy without violence. It is this very lack of love—this deeply unimaginative moment—that leads to chants of "blood and soil" and "Jews will not replace us" wherein the forced intimacy of living beside or in the same nation as the other must always result in violence. Baldwin and others hold up a radical form of love as an affective and embodied mode by which we become vulnerable to the other, and we are able to see in others (and ourselves) good along with bad.

This love can grow from our disgust, from a disappointed love, and/or from the wounds of rejected vulnerability. To be faced, again and again, with violence, with oppression, and with denigration may result in anger or rage. But such rage and anger, if unmodified, are profoundly destructive. Summarizing Baldwin's thinking about love and rage, Sean Kim Butorac (2018) writes this: "Love that suppresses or denies anger is shallow and inauthentic, while anger that makes no recourse to love becomes self-destructive and impotent" (p. 717).

And so we are disgusted. But we also have love. We love those who stand shoulder to shoulder with us at marches and rallies, with colleagues and friends and strangers who share our commitments to a more just, less racist, less misogynistic, more welcoming world. More—and far more difficultly—we love, as well, so many who feel betrayed by the nation, and left out of the promises made to them and in their rage take up the easiest available affective structure—white rage. We are always appalled by and opposed to this solution, for it privileges the destructiveness of rage, and seeks the destruction of all humans who seem different. And yet, all of us, as Cornell West said immediately after Charlottesville, are filled with hatred (Platt 2017). In our own public lives, we strive (not always successfully) to resist divisive affects and to weave the energy of our disgust with the affiliative passion of social love.

We were struck, as we were writing this conclusion, by a short story on NPR about the old American song "This Little Light of Mine" (Deggans 2018). Early in the radio essay, Deggans plays the soundtrack of a group of counter-protestors in Charlottesville. As the white nationalist marchers move past chanting "you will not replace us" and "Jews will not replace us" the counter-protesters break out in the simple song "this little light of mine, I'm going to let it shine." Reverend Osagyefo Sekou, one of the counter-protestors, recalls that the white nationalists were shaken. "They didn't know what to do with all that joy. We weren't going to let the darkness have the last word" (Deggans 2018). Against the identity-based, purifying rhetoric of "we will not be replaced," the counter-protestors humbly recognized that their light, while little, still shines, and, when combined with other little lights, dispels darkness. Disgust combines with hope, with compassion, and with an ability to see in each of us the possibilities of hatred but also the possibility of transcending hatred with morally infused compassion.

As is, no doubt, evident by this point, we are disgusted—reasonably, we believe—by Trump's authoritarian, narcissistic, racist rhetoric. Rather than attempt to hide that disgust, we have featured it prominently throughout this book. For some readers, that choice will likely be regarded as a serious and perhaps even disqualifying shortcoming of the preceding analysis. We are, after all, taught to strive for objectivity in our work, to pretend that our scholarship is free from political bias.

This, of course, is not—and never has been—the case. It is the prevailing, if not exclusive, academic style, however. The choice to reject this style in favor of a different aesthetic reflects a deliberate attempt on our part to tap into a broader cultural sensibility of disgust. But, at the same time, we are writing out of a deeply held and passionate commitment to hope. We hope that if we can bring together reasonable disgust at the materially consequential rhetorical style of Donald Trump with the affiliative and fierce force of love, then we can turn back from the brink of totalitarianism.

We are not, as has become apparent, political theorists but simple rhetorical critics. Our task here has been to carefully but passionately engage a rhetorical affectivity that we believe could destroy the nation and is, on a daily basis, harming millions of people in the US and elsewhere. We have done so because we believe in the power of rhetorical criticism to shine a little light onto increasingly totalitarian rhetorical practice. We offer our own disgust and our own compassionate love as the motivation for writing this book and as the basis of our (often dim) hope. We have focused on Trump's rhetoric as a particularly insidious version of white rage. Our disgust is directed not at Trump, but at the racism, misogyny, homophobia, and xenophobia that his rhetoric both draws upon and extends. Our hope is bigger than simply electing a different president. Instead, we join James Baldwin (1993) in a grander, riskier, and more important goal—that is to "to end our racial nightmare, and achieve our country, and change the history of the world." "If we do not dare everything," he continues, "the fulfillment of that prophecy, re-created from the Bible in song by a slave, is upon us: *God gave Noah the rainbow sign, No more water, the fire next time*" (pp. 105–106).

Our hope is to have written a book that is not only insightful—one that illuminates how Trump's managerial, physical, and linguistic style was central to his rhetorical appeal and how he mobilized Twitter to maximize that appeal—but also one that is moving, charged with affect, that resonates with disgust *and* love so that we might better overcome the very grave threat that confronts us all.

Note

1. *As support for Foer's position, consider* Jill Filopovic's *argument that* "President Trump ran a campaign of aggrieved masculinity, appealing to men who felt their rightful place in society has been taken from them by a stream of immigrants stealing their jobs, women who don't need husbands to support them, and members of minority groups who don't work as hard but still get special treatment" (Filopovic 2017).

References

Baldwin, J. 1993. *The fire next time*. New York: Vintage Books.

Biskupic, J. 2018. Trump's sustained attacks on American rights. *CNN.com* [online]. Available at: www.cnn.com/2018/05/26/politics/trump-rights-due-process-curiel/index.html [Accessed August 30, 2018].

Boutrac, S. K. 2018. Hannah Arendt, James Baldwin, and the politics of love. *Political Research Quarterly*, 71(3), pp. 710–721.

Burke, K. 1937. *Attitudes toward history*, 3rd ed. Berkeley: University of California Press.

Burnucca, C. 2017. 7 racist things Trump said in 2017 that'll make you so disappointed. *EliteDaily* [online]. Available at: www.elitedaily.com/p/7-racist-things-trump-said-in-2017-thatll-make-you-so-disappointed-7679277 [Accessed August 30, 2018].

Cauterucci, C. 2017. Trump's boy scouts speech is a reminder of how different the Girls Scouts Organization is. *Slate* [online]. Available at: www.slate.com/blogs/xx_factor/2017/07/25/the_boy_scouts_loved_trump_s_speech_reminding_us_how_different_girl_scouts.html [Accessed May 2, 2018].

Cose, E. 2018. One year after Charlottesville, Trump has normalized racism in America. *USA Today* [online]. Available at: www.usatoday.com/story/opinion/2018/08/10/white-supremacists-neo-nazis-charlottesville-unite-right-rally-trump-column/935708002/ [Accessed August 10, 2018].

Decker, C. 2017. Trump's war against elites and expertise. *Los Angeles Times* [online]. Available at: www.latimes.com/politics/la-na-pol-trump-elites-20170725-story.html [Accessed March 7, 2018].

Devega, C, 2016a. Secrets of Donald Trump's cult. *Salon* [online]. Available at: www.salon.com/2016/02/06/secrets_of_donald_trumps_cult_this_is_why_the_angriest_white_voters_will_not_leave_his_side/ [Accessed November 15, 2017].

Devega, C. 2016b. Donald Trump's rageful white cult: Race, fear and the GOP front-runner's slick manipulations. *Salon* [online]. Available at: www.salon.com/2016/02/22/donald_trumps_rageful_white_cult_race_fear_and_the_gop_front_runners_slick_manipulations/ [Accessed August 20, 2018].

Dyson, E. M. 2017. *Tears we cannot stop: A sermon to white America*. New York: St. Martin's Press.

Edwards-Levy, A. 2017. Trump supporters now less likely to think they're losing ground in America. *HuffPost* [online]. Available at: www.huffingtonpost.com/entry/trump-clinton-supporters-poll-life-better-worse_us_59161b74e4b00f308cf542cc [Accessed January 9, 2018].

Filopovic, J. 2017. The all-male photo op isn't a gaffe. It's a strategy. *New York Times* [online]. Available at: www.nytimes.com/2017/03/27/opinion/the-all-male-photo-op-isnt-a-gaffe-its-a-strategy.html [Accessed April 25, 2018].

Foer, F. 2016. Donald Trump hates women. *Slate* [online]. Available at: www.slate.com/articles/news_and_politics/politics/2016/03/donald_trump_has_one_core_philosophy_misogyny.html [Accessed August 30, 2018].

Goldberg, M. 2017. "They believe the government is now on their side." *Slate* [online]. Available at: www.slate.com/articles/news_and_politics/politics/2017/07/louisville_s_last_abortion_clinic_is_a_battleground_for_the_militant_anti.html [Accessed August 30, 2018].

Grewal, D. 2018. Do Trump tweets spur hate crimes? *Scientific American* [online]. Available at: www.scientificamerican.com/article/do-trump-tweets-spur-hate-crimes1/ [Accessed August 30, 2018].

Hannin, E. 2018. Trump administration is trying to systematically strip citizenship from many Americans born near Mexico border. *Slate* [online]. Available at: https://slate.com/news-and-politics/2018/08/trump-administration-trying-to-strip-citizenship-from-americans-born-near-mexico-border.html [Accessed 30 August 30, 2018].

Hook. D. 2006. 'Pre-discursive' racism. *Journal of Community & Applied Social Psychology*, 16(3), pp. 207–232.

Kayam, O. 2018. The readability and simplicity of Donald Trump's language. *Critical Studies Review*, 16(1), pp. 73–88.

Marcotte, A. 2016. Conservatism turned toxic: Donald Trump's fanbase has no actual ideology, just a nihilistic hatred of liberals. *Salon* [online]. Available at: www.salon.com/2016/12/23/conservatism-turned-toxic-donald-trumps-fanbase-has-no-actual-ideology-just-a-nihilistic-hatred-of-liberals/ [Accessed August 31, 2017].

McElwee, S. and McDaniel, J. 2017. Economic anxiety didn't make people vote Trump. *The Nation* [online]. Available at: www.thenation.com/article/economic-anxiety-didnt-make-people-vote-trump-racism-did/ [Accessed June 9, 2018].

NAACP. 2018. NAACP sees continued rise in hate crimes, legacy of Trump's racism, NAACP.org [online]. Available at: www.naacp.org/latest/naacp-sees-continued-rise-hate-crimes-legacy-trumps-racism/ [Accessed August 30, 2018].

Obeidallah, D. 2018. Trump channels inner dictator, calls for Samantha Bee to be fired. *DailyBeast* [online]. Available at: www.thedailybeast.com/trump-channels-inner-dictator-calls-for-samantha-bee-to-be-fired [Accessed August 30, 2018].

Posner, S. 2017. Amazing disgrace. *New Republic* [online]. Available at: https://newrepublic.com/article/140961/amazing-disgrace-donald-trump-hijacked-religious-right> [Accessed 15 July 15, 2018].

Samaha, A. 2017. We found 81 incidents of Trump-inspired bullying that happened last school year. *BuzzFeed* [online]. Available at: www.buzzfeed.com/albertsamaha/we-found-dozens-more-incidents-of-trump-inspired-bullying?utm_term=.gvQPOZOk1#.ctr7E4Eyg [Accessed April 20, 2018].

Sunstein, C. R. 2017. Yes, Trump is making xenophobia more acceptable. *Bloomberg* [online]. Available at: www.bloomberg.com/view/articles/2017-05-26/yes-trump-is-making-xenophobia-more-acceptable [Accessed January 30, 2017].

Tompkins, S. 1995. *Exploring affect: The selected writings of Silvan S. Tompkins*, ed. E. V. Demos. Cambridge: Cambridge University Press.
Yancy, G. 2015. Dear White America. *New York Times* [online]. Available at: https://opinionator.blogs.nytimes.com/2015/12/24/dear-white-america/ [Accessed August 8, 2018].

Index